HOW TO FIND YOUR FAMILY ROOTS

by
William Latham

Published by:
SANTA MONICA PRESS
P.O. Box 1076
Santa Monica, CA 90406-1076

Printed in the United States

Library of Congress Cataloging-in-Publication Data

Latham, William, 1942-
How to Find Your Family Roots: The Complete Guide to Searching for Your Ancestors / William Latham
New! Expanded Edition
224 pp
ISBN 0-9639946-0-3
Library of Congress Catalog Card Number 93-87392
1. United States -- Genealogy -- Handbooks, manuals, etc.
929.1L

10 9 8 7 6 5 4 3 2

CONTENTS

1

INTRODUCTION

The Excitement of Finding Your Family Roots

Have you ever wondered if one of your ancestors were a famous, important person? A President, or even a King or a Queen? Perhaps your last name is Washington, and you've always thought that perhaps you were a distant relative of the father of our country. If you've shown a flair for painting or writing, maybe you've fantasized that you inherited your talent from an ancestor with a name like Michaelangelo or Shakespeare.

Certainly, the heritage of each and every one of us is a fascinating topic. Who hasn't dreamed of origins, of people living in another place, in another time? Who hasn't seen an old photograph of a person to whom they bear a striking resemblance and thought, "I wonder if . . ?"

In this book, I will show you how the process of finding your family roots—known as "genealogy"—can act as a kind of time machine or magic carpet that allows you to travel back into the past. Once there, you can find out information that has helped to shape who you are—not only in terms of your physical appearance, but your personality, beliefs, habits, and skills as well. Additionally, this search for your roots will take you through time and space, from century to century and from state to state or even exotic country to country. Your search will give you a greater sense of exactly how you fit into this giant web of people and places that we call the history of mankind. And what's more, I'll show you how to do all of this in a simple, easy, and inexpensive manner.

How to Find Your Family Roots is not some academic report filled with complicated research techniques and impossible suggestions and instructions. Instead, I have written this book for people like you and me.

People who are naturally curious. People who care about their family, who care about their heritage and want to find out valuable information and share it with other members of their clan and pass it on to future generations. You'll find that it's not only easy to find out a great deal of information about your family roots, it's also a lot of fun! Think of it like a giant jigsaw puzzle, of which you, your family, and your ancestors are the pieces!!

Definition and History of Genealogy

The term "genealogy" actually comes from two Greek words: "genea," which means "race" or "family"; and "logia," which means "science" or "study of." When we speak of the science of genealogy, we are really talking about the study of the descent of a person or of a family.

The science of genealogy is as old as the Bible, which serves as the first written example of genealogy. Ancient civilizations, such as the Greeks, showed a keen interest in genealogy—as displayed in the works of Homer and the plays of Aeschylus and Euripedes. Another early use of genealogy was to prove that a person was descended from either certain Gods and Goddesses or from particular Kings and Queens. Therefore, up until the 16th century the science of genealogy was most often used by either rulers or the upper classes. In the 16th century, extensive written records began to be kept, thus making it far easier for ordinary citizens to trace back their lineage.

Any way you look at it, interest in man's lineage is as old as civilized man himself.

9

What You Will Accomplish

As you begin the task of unraveling the mystery of your family's origin, you will learn a great deal about the history of both America and the World, as well as about geography, people and their lifestyles, and most importantly, yourself—who you are and where you come from.

Ideally, you should be able to trace your roots back to the original paternal and maternal immigrants of your family—most likely your grandparents or great-grandparents, but in some instances, maybe even further than that. If you are able to do this, you will know your complete American genealogy and you should congratulate yourself—most people do not know this much about their family. Your next step would be to try and trace your lineage to the forefathers of your family's original immigrants, to those who were born and those who died in some far away country hundreds of years ago. Finally, you will take whatever information you have gathered and write a letter, report, or even a book about your discoveries. Some enthusiasts even form a family organization that meets once or twice a year, bringing together relatives that they have never met or possibly didn't even know existed.

But even if you are only able to go back two or three generations, even if you only come up with a handful of dates, names and places, you will have accomplished a great deal, something of which you can be especially proud. Why? Because you will have the satisfaction of knowing that you have set up a solid foundation for the future generations of your family. You will have set a precedent that will surely inspire one of your descendants to pick up the ball and continue the project you started. Additionally, by providing a written record of your lineage, you will give those around you and those who will follow in your footsteps immeasurable joy in knowing just who they are and where they come from.

Perhaps I am getting a little too serious here. The main thing you must keep in mind while tracing your family tree is to have fun! Because it's not about how far back you are able to go or how complete a family history you are able to put together. No, it's really about getting in touch with relatives you haven't talked to in a long time or have never even met. It's about finding long lost mementos and hearing old family tales that have been buried in the memories of your older relatives for years and years because nobody was ever truly interested enough to ask them to tell these stories. It's about all of this and much, much more . . . .

And remember, the sooner you get started, the better. Your relatives are not getting any younger, and once they are gone, their memories and their stories will go with them. Don't let time pass you by, leaving you in the unenviable position of kicking yourself while you cry, "If only I would've talked to him while he was alive!" So what are you waiting for? Let's begin your search for your family roots!

2

A BRIEF HISTORY
OF AMERICA'S IMMIGRANTS

From Many Lands, for Many Reasons

Beginning with those who sailed to America aboard the Mayflower in 1620, the first immigrants who came to our country were primarily from England. In the early part of the 18th century, the Germans, Scottish, and Irish began crossing over, and by the end of the 1700s, there were close to five million people living in the United States. With the exception of three quarters of a million black African slaves, the vast majority of the people living in the United States at this time were from one of these four original countries.

By the mid-1800s, people from all over the world, including Ireland, France, Switzerland, China, and Japan, began immigrating to the United States. And between 1880 and the early part of the 20th century, over 15 million southern and eastern Europeans came to sample and savor the riches of America.

Aside from the economic opportunities, immigrants sought out America as a refuge from religious persecution, political oppression and a host of other reasons—including broken hearts, wanderlust, and the attraction of the unknown.

The Harrowing Voyage Across the Ocean

Virtually every European immigrant left from one of two sea ports, both of which were located in Germany—at Hamburg and Bremen. These ports were very seedy and there were many wicked and evil people looking to take advantage of the frightened and lonely travelers. Perhaps it is partly because of this that most immigrants arrived in the United States with less than 25 dollars in their pockets.

As far as the journey across the ocean was concerned, it was, in the early days anyway, an extremely rough and uncomfortable trip. A typical passenger would be crammed into a tiny cabin with perhaps a half dozen other travelers. Rarely would anybody ever complete the whole journey without having experienced at least one bout of seasickness.

Some days a ship might sail at a rate of as much as eight miles an hour, but other times the passengers could end up further from their future home than they were when they had awoke at dawn.

The length of the voyages varied from a little over a month to well over four months, bringing even more uncertainty to the already frightened travelers. At times, groups of ships would sail together, and members of the crew as well as passengers could visit other ships. Other times, however, days would pass without another ship in sight.

Many dangers, ranging from mean-spirited Pirates who roamed the open seas, to fierce storms which pounded the planks of the ships, also contributed to the overall hardship of the journey. But when all was said and done, once the immigrants set foot on American soil, they forgot the troubles that the trip had wrought, and looked forward to a new beginning and a new lease on life.

Before Ellis Island was built in 1892, immigrants were processed at Castle Garden, located at the far tip of Manhattan. Asian immigrants used to be processed at the Pacific Mail Steamship Company warehouse in San Francisco, but after 1910 they were welcomed at Angel Island in San Francisco Bay.

Crossing the Country

Once landed on the east coast of America, early English immigrants would typically settle in one of two places—Massachusetts and Virginia. By the mid-

15

17th century, immigrants from an assortment of countries would often take uncomfortable and even punishing stagecoach rides on the King's Highway to Philadelphia, Pennsylvania. Many would then continue on to Norfolk, Virginia, and even as far south as Charleston, South Carolina. In later years, an immigrant could grab a stage coach in Philadelphia and take the Great Road out west towards Kentucky.

By the middle of the 1800s, roads began reaching further and further into the South and the West, taking new citizens to exotic far off places like New Orleans, Santa Fe, and throughout California. While the roads were tough, and the journey was rough, our forefathers bit the bullet and not only survived but triumphed with a dignity and a pride that has since gone on to be associated with the word, "American."

3

STARTING YOUR SEARCH FOR YOUR FAMILY ROOTS

Pen, Pencil and Paper

The only tools that are really required when you begin searching out your family roots are a pen, pencil, and small notepad. If you can afford to purchase a hand-held micro-cassette recorder, I highly recommend doing so. These small tape recorders eliminate the need to take copious notes during interviews. They are unobtrusive (once the interview begins you and your subject will forget that it is even there), and they allow you to concentrate on what your subject has to say. You'll find more on this matter in chapter five.

A ready supply of sharpened pencils and couple of ball point pens are obviously necessary, as is a small, pocket-size notepad. This notepad is important to have so that you can jot down notes, thoughts, hints, tips and the like. Valuable information can be obtained at any time, in any place, and you'll want to have a convenient place to write down the facts as opposed to relying on your memory.

Organizing Your Research Material

As you begin searching out your family roots, you will undoubtedly begin to gather a great deal of material, ranging from charts and documents to mementos and family photos. In order to keep track of everything, it is imperative that you put together some type of filing system. If you do not do this, you will end up with a morass of notes and papers, scattered about everywhere, making it virtually impossible for you to find necessary items which could be crucial to continuing your search.

Before getting into the particulars of a filing system, let me first go over the major documents with which you will be working. These are the Ancestral Charts and the Family Group Charts.

Ancestral Charts (See figure 1)

A ancestral is the record of a line of ancestors. The first ancestral chart you will work with will go back four generations, to approximately the middle of the 1800s. As you move along in your search, you will be filling out the ancestral chart to mark your progress. It's probably a good idea to fill out this chart in pencil, in order to facilitate any changes you may have to make as you go along.

There is a basic, standard format which any genealogist, professional or amateur, follows when filling out ancestral charts. This format helps you keep all of your charts consistent and very easy to read, which is important when you want to access some information from them in a hurry.

Starting with yourself, record each member's full name, placing every letter of each surname in capitals. For example, ADAMS. Alice Jill. Next, write down the month, day and year this person was born. For example, March 18, 1953. After that comes the place of birth, which should include the city and state (and, if you have room, the county). For example, Kansas City, Missouri. You may use the standard two letter abbreviation for the state if you wish. Continue this format for the dates and places of marriages and deaths. If you are not sure about a fact, you should place a question mark in parenthesis following the questionable information.

Numbering System

When filling out ancestral charts, you should assign each member a number. Then, all materials which relate to individual family members will be filed under this same number. The easiest way to go about doing this is to begin with yourself, assigning the num-

Figure 1
Ancestral Chart (Three Generation)

4

Name: ADAMS, Joseph
Born: April 5, 1905
Place: Chicago, IL
Married: October 7, 1927
Place: Chicago, IL
Died: July 17, 1977
Place: Kansas City, MO

2

Name: ADAMS, John L.
Born: June 9, 1930
Place: Kansas City, MO
Married: May 10, 1955
Place: Kansas City, MO
Died: July 17, 1989
Place: Phoenix, AZ

5

Name: BARR, Mary Alice
Born: June 27, 1910
Place: Chicago, IL
Married: October 7, 1927
Place: Chicago, IL
Died: February 3, 1962
Place: Kansas City, MO

1

Name: ADAMS, Alice Jill
Born: March 18, 1953
Place: Kansas City, MO
Married: May 14, 1973
Place: Santa Monica, CA

6

Name: TULLEY, Walter
Born: January 15, 1899
Place: Boston, MA
Married: June 23, 1937
Place: Detroit, MI
Died: September 8, 1965
Place: Dallas, TX

3

Name: TULLEY, Eunice
Born: April 1, 1938
Place: Detroit, MI
Married: October 3, 1955
Place: Kansas City, MO

7

Name: CLARK, Lucy Ann
Born: March 30, 1918
Place: Detroit, MI
Married: June 23, 1937
Place: Detroit, MI
Married: May 14, 1969
Place: Santa Monica, CA

20

ber 1 to your name. Number 2 will then go to your father, number 3 to your mother and so on. To further facilitate your records, only assign even numbers to males, and odd numbers to females. Therefore, number 4 will be you paternal grandfather (your father's father), number 5 your paternal grandmother (your father's mother), number 6 your maternal grandfather (your mother's father), number 7 your maternal grandmother (your mother's mother), etc. While this may initially seem to be slightly confusing, in the long run you will find that it actually makes all of your record keeping exceedingly clear and concise.

Family Group Chart
   (See figure 2)
   Along with your ancestral chart, the family group chart is your bread and butter, the primary tool with which you will continually be working. Filling out this sheet, as you can see, is relatively simple. There are one or two things to keep in mind however. First, while two and three marriages per individual is not all that common in the late twentieth century, in earlier times you will undoubtedly come across many family members who were married more than once, primarily because the much rougher and tougher lifestyle (along with the lack of modern medical research) often led to early deaths of one partner or another. Therefore, be aware that you must keep a separate family group chart for each marriage.
   Most importantly, try to be extremely accurate when placing any information onto these charts. Any error could prove to be very costly, leading you into hours of research which will ultimately prove to be thoroughly needless and unwarranted. If, for instance, you place a wrong first name for one of the children,

21

Figure 2
Family Group Chart

Husband's Code Number _____

	Husband	Wife
Name		
Date of Birth		
Place of Birth		
Father's Name		
Mother's Name		
Date of Marriage		
Place of Marriage		
Date of Death		
Place of Death		

Children

Name	Born	Place	Died	Place

Family Residences

City	County	State	Dates

you could begin searching somebody's life who isn't even a member of your family. Therefore, always be sure to check and double check your facts and figures.

Filing System

Now we come to the final portion of the "setting up" period of your search for your family roots, namely the aforementioned filing system. Because each family group chart is tagged with the number of the husband (or head of the family), they will be filed according to the numerical sequence 2,4,6,8,10...(with the possible addition of number 1 if the genealogist himself is the head of a family).

In addition to the family group chart files, I also recommend that you keep a miscellaneous file. Into this file will go smaller files, arranged by family group chart code numbers, which contain photographs, diaries, wills, newspaper clippings and any thing else which pertains to a certain family member. This file is absolutely essential in order to ensure that you don't end up with piles of bits and pieces of information.

You may also want to keep a file titled "Dead End" for any leads and sources of information that ultimately led nowhere. You never know when such information may come into play somewhere down the line, and keeping this research together in one place will make it easy to find should you ever suddenly have use for it.

Now let's go through and see how your filing system and family group charts will operate. Say that you want to look up all the information that you have collected about your paternal grandfather (your father's father). To begin with, you will notice that on the ancestral chart, he has been assigned the number of 4. You would then go to the family group chart that is also numbered 4, and the miscellaneous file which, obviously, is also marked with the number 4.

If, for instance, you wanted to look up your paternal grandmother's brothers and sisters, you would go to the family group chart that is numbered 10. Why? Because, as you can see from the ancestral chart, your paternal grandmother's father has been assigned the number 10, and therefore all information about your grandmother's brothers and sisters will be contained on the family group chart which corresponds with your grandmother's father's code number, or number 10. As you can see, this system is efficient and fairly simple to follow once you get going.

And that's exactly what you are now prepared to do. With an excellent record-keeping system at your disposal, you are now ready to plunge ahead into the wonderful and exciting world of "ancestor hunting." So, with this out of the way, let's go . . . .

4

NAMES, RELATIONSHIPS AND DATES: EARLY KEYS TO YOUR SEARCH

Names

Your family name is the most basic, fundamental element of your genealogical quest. Like a fingerprint, a name is a personal marking that offers the first clue as to who you are and where you came from. By understanding the origins, history, and meaning of names, you will be able to uncover a remarkable amount of information—the town where an ancestor was born, their occupation, religion, cultural ties, class status, and even their personality or physical characteristics!

Their Origins and Meanings

The original Anglo-Saxon names of about 5,000 years ago had little or no meaning at all. Many of these names, such as Clovis and Begga, did not make a distinction between males and females. But with the Norman Conquest of 1066, the English and Europeans began using the Norman names—Richard, Robert, etc.—that remain familiar to us hundreds of years later.

The Normans, however, only used a handful of names and, with an increasing population, citizens living in the Middle Ages found themselves running short of choices. It was at this point that the Church stepped in and began suggesting that people use Saints' names, and so Stephen, Elizabeth, Katherine, and others immediately became popular. It was also at this time that people began to add descriptions to their names in order to distinguish themselves from family, friends, neighbors, and fellow townspeople with the same name. These descriptions usually had to do with an individual's physical characteristics or the place were they lived, such as Robert The Bald or John The Pious.

26

By the 14th or 15th century, surnames had become extremely common and, as with given names, they often described what someone looked like or where they lived. If Richard was not a tall man, he might be called Richard Short. Everard, who lived in Hungerford, was known as Everard de Hungerford. Personal characteristics and occupations also began to be reflected in a person's name. John Moody or Thomas Dull obviously had moody and dull personalities respectively. Weaver, Farmer, Miller, and Baker were common surnames denoting occupations.

Finally, relationships were often designated within surnames via the practice known as patronymics. Such names point out that an individual was the son or descendant of a particular person. For example, MacGregor is Scottish for "the son of Gregory," while Mendelssohn is German for the "son of Mendel." In English, one sees patronymics at work in the last names of Johnson, Jackson, and Peterson. However, when patronymics first began to be used, the surname would change with every generation. Thus, John the son of Peter would be called John Peterson. But John's son, Robert, would be known as Robert Johnson. Henry V came along and effectively put an end to this confusing practice when, in 1413, he ordered that everyone begin using their surnames on all legal documents. By the middle of the 16th century, family names had become stabilized and surnames derived from patronymics remained the same from generation to generation.

There are many excellent books available that deal exclusively with the history of names, or "onomatology." J.N. Hook's *Family Names: How Our Surnames Came to America*, Elsdon C. Smith's *American Surnames*, and P.H. Reaney's *Dictionary of British*

Surnames are all highly recommended.

Did Your Ancestor Change His Name?

It is estimated that there are over 1.5 million last names currently in use in the United States. This may sound like a large number, but it is actually relatively small when you think about the tremendous amount of immigrants who have brought vast numbers of Western and Eastern European names into the country.

Why is this? Basically because immigrants to this country often changed their name—or were given a new name—when they entered the United States. This resulted in many new citizens taking similar names. In fact, the most common names in America today—Smith, Jones, Johnson, Brown, etc.—are virtually the same as they were around the time of the American Revolution. The name "Smith" provides a good example of how this worked. Immigrants from many different countries whose name meant "blacksmith"—for example the German "Schmidt" or the Italian "Ferraro"—adopted the name "Smith" when they reached the shores of America. Thus, what was already a popular, although variously spelled and pronounced, name in many different countries was suddenly funneled into one name in America. The result being an enormous amount of people having the same name and making that name extraordinarily popular for all succeeding generations.

The changing of an immigrant's name was done for a wide variety of reasons. Your ancestor may have changed his surname in an attempt to "Americanize" the name. For instance, many German immigrants discovered that Americans had trouble pronouncing their names, and so "Koch" became "Cook" and

"Albrecht" became "Allbright."

It was even more common, however, for the change in name to be the result of a decision made by an immigration official. This was especially true in the case of Polish immigrants. Someone from Poland with a name such as "Marcizszewski" would come through, and out of confusion or simply laziness, the immigration official would change the spelling to the closest English sound he could come up with on the spot—in this case, "Muskie." Welfare agencies and churchmen back in an immigrant's native country were also often to blame for the change in spelling, as were, strangely enough, our ancestors themselves! Daniel Boone, for example, was known to have signed his name "Bone" and "Boon" in addition to the more familiar (to us anyway) "Boone." Federal census takers were also notoriously inept at recording the correct spelling of names, and the census of 1790 finds even simple names spelled dozens of different ways. Here are several examples of common names and the variations you would likely encounter if you were searching for one of them:

Brown: Bronn, Broons, Broune, Browne.
Bailey: Bailie, Bailly, Baillie, Baily, Baley.
Carl: Carle, Karl, Karle.
Frank: Franc, Franck, Franke, Franks.
Madison: Maddison, Matheson, Matsen, Matson, Mattison, Mattson.
Meyer: Mayer, Meier, Meyers, Mier, Myer.
Reynolds: Ranals, Renholds, Reynull, Rynolds.

While name variants may not at first seem to be important, they are actually crucial when searching for you family roots. Remember, you will be looking through all kinds of public records. If you aren't aware of the different spellings of your ancestor's surnames, you may very well overlook key pieces of information that could unlock the door which leads to a whole new branch of your family tree.

How to Search for a Changed Name

Searching for your ancestors would be a much easier task if the spelling of last names remained consistent throughout the centuries, but unfortunately that is not the case. Don't despair though, for there are many ways to overcome this small hurdle. The first thing to do is to sit down and think of all of the different ways you can possibly spell your last name. (For instance, if your last name is "Kane," you might write "Cain," "Cane," "Caine," "Kain," "Kaine," and "Kaines.") Sometimes, saying your name out loud a few times will help you think of other possibilities. Try to mispronounce your name to see if that raises additional spellings. And remember to include the spellings and pronunciations that other people have mistakenly used during your lifetime.

Once you begin actively searching for your family roots, you will discover many other ways to find out either your ancestor's original name or a spelling variant. In cemeteries, you'll often find the original, pre-immigration surname on the tombstone, as many of our ancestor's chose to be buried with their original name as opposed to the one they either adopted or were forced to adopt upon landing in the United States. Death certificates might also contain an ancestor's original name. If you by chance come across several death certificates from members of one family, and one of the certificates contains a different spelling of—or even a completely different—last name, don't dismiss it as a clerical error. That ancestor may have given you a valuable clue through his choice to be buried with his original name.

One of the most common occurrences of name changes can be seen with occupational names. If you or one of your ancestors has this type of name, the name change may be easy to identify. Here are several examples:

Occupational Name Changes

English	French	German	Italian	Polish
Baker	Boulanger	Becker	Fornari	Piekarz
Carpente	Charpentier	Schreiner	Martello	Cieslak
Farmer	Gagnon	Bauer		Kmiec
Fisher		Fischer	Pisciolo	Ryback
Miller	Meunier	Muller	Farina	
Priest		Pabst	Prete	Kaplan
Shepherd	Berger	Schaefer	Pecora	
Taylor	Tailleur	Schneider	Sartori	Krawczyk

While you might be thinking that coming up with a half-dozen different ways to spell your name will only make your search that much more complicated, let me assure you it will not. Remember that you will usually have other information available at your disposal, such as birthdates, birthplaces, dates of death, place of burial, etc., which will help you to narrow your search a great deal.

Relationships

While our relationships to our parents, brothers, sisters, and children are relatively simple to understand, and while most of us have a firm grasp of our relationship to cousins, aunts, uncles, and grandparents, anything more distant can get confusing. Yet, when searching for your family's roots, you must have a firm grasp of relationships if you expect to put together an accurate family tree. Additionally, if you

31

erroneously claim an individual as your ancestor, and then begin to trace his roots, you will have wasted a great deal of time and energy. Here are a few tips and hints that I hope will help clear up much of the relationship puzzle:

1) The first thing you should know about relationships is the distinction between "direct" ancestors and "collateral" relatives. A direct ancestor's name will appear on your ancestral chart—your father, mother, grandparents, great-grandparents, etc. A collateral relative will only appear on family group charts as either brothers or sisters of your direct relatives, or as descendants of your aunts and uncles.

2) Aside from direct and collateral relationships, there are also "in-laws," and "step," "half" and "adoptive" relationships. "In-laws" are related by marriage; they are the ancestors and relatives of a spouse. "Step" relationships occur when a man or woman with children remarries. If a woman with a boy remarries a man who has no children, then the man becomes the boy's stepfather, and all of the man's relatives become steprelatives to the boy. If the woman and the man have a daughter together, the new baby girl becomes a "half" sister to the little boy. When researching adoptive situations, you should realize that, rightly or wrongly, many hereditary and lineage societies will not accept adopted descendants as members, even though they may have all of the legal rights of heirs.

3) In order to simplify your records, succeeding generations of great-grandparents should be identified as 2nd great-grandfather (or grandmother), 3rd great-grandfather, etc. Grandsons and granddaughters should also be identified by this same system, as 2nd great-grandson (or granddaughter), 3rd great-grandson, etc.

4) It is probably clear to most of you that a cousin is the child of your uncle or aunt (your father or mother's brother or sister's child). Confusion tends to set in, however, when the term cousin is applied to someone more remotely related who still shares a common ancestor. In these instances, terms such as second cousin and third cousin, or third cousin once removed begin to enter into the genealogical picture. The following chart should help to clear up any confusion caused by such terms and relationships.

	Ron Jones	
Steve Jones	brothers	Rick Jones
Brian Jones	cousins	Cindy Jones
Matthew Jones	2nd cousins	Kevin Smith
Jordan Jones	3rd cousins	Brent Smith
	3c1r	Jeffrey Smith
	3c2r	Diana Smith

In this example, you can see that Ron Jones had two sons—Rick and Steve. Rick Jones fathered Cindy Jones. Cindy Jones then married a man by the last name of Smith, and they had a son named Kevin. Kevin Smith then had a son named Brent, who in turn fathered Jeffrey and Diana. On the other side of the tree, Steve Jones had a son named Brian, who fathered Matthew, who in turn fathered Jordan. However, Jordan Jones (who is Brent Smith's third cousin) did not have any children. Therefore, because Jeffrey Smith and Jordan Jones are separated by a generation, they are considered to be third cousins once removed. Similarly, Diana Smith and Jordan Jones are 3rd cousins twice removed. Please note the abbreviations used for such relationships, i.e. 3c1r (third cousin once removed), 3c2r (third cousin twice removed) and so forth—they will come in handy when you are keeping your family records.

5) Believe it or not, the cousin relationship becomes even more confusing when we go back in history. During the 17th century, for instance, the term "cousin" was applied to any relative who wasn't a brother, sister, son, or daughter. Grandchildren, nephews and nieces, uncles and aunts—these relatives were often referred to as "cousins" in wills and other legal documents. Similarly, stepchildren (a spouse's child by a former marriage) were often referred to as a "son-in-law" or "daughter-in-law," while "son" and "daughter" were used in place of the 20th century meaning we assign to the terms "son-in-law" and "daughter-in-law."

"Brother" can also prove to be a tricky term in historical documents. Aside from the definition we tend to use—that of a blood brother, or one who shares the same parents as ourselves—"brother" often meant "brother-in-law," "stepbrother," or a "church brother." Likewise, "father" and "mother" often stood for who we tend to think of as "father-in-law," "mother-in-law," "stepfather," or "stepmother."

The last source of confusion that you may come across as you move back through the centuries concerns the use of "Mrs." "Mrs." often stood for "Mistriss," which was a term of social distinction. The woman may or may not have been married.

When researching your family roots, make sure that you pay close attention to the terms used to describe relationships in wills, birth and death certificates, and other legal documents. Never take anything at face value. Look at other familial records for collaboration before accepting a new member into your family

Dates

When searching through records which refer to any year prior to 1752, you might come across some dates that look peculiar. Perhaps the most common puzzler is the appearance of "Old Style" or "New Style" (often abbreviated to O.S. and N.S.) following a date, and of the practice known as "double dating." No, I'm not talking about when two couples go out together for the evening! This type of double dating refers to the custom of using two years when citing a date of birth or death. For instance, if you were searching for George Washington's date of birth you might find a record which has it written as February 11, 1731/2. Or, you might see it recorded somewhere else as February 11, 1731, Old Style or February 22, 1732, New Style.

Double-dating, and the use of Old Style and New Style following the date, occurs because of a change that was originally made to the calendar in 1582, and finally adopted by the English in 1752. Prior to 1582, the Julian calendar—established by Julius Caesar in 46 B.C.—was the favored calendar of the Christian world. According to this calendar, the year was divided into 365 days, and every fourth (or leap) year there would be an extra day. However, in 1582, it was discovered that every 400 years the Julian calendar was three days ahead of the actual time as dictated by the earth's revolution around the sun. By 1582, this translated into ten extra days. If this remained unchecked, the months of the year and the seasons which we normally associate with them—for instance August with summer or February with winter—would no longer match. More importantly, the date of the vernal equinox had shifted from March 21 to March 11, and the dates for Easter had been thrown out of sorts. Appropriately, the Roman Catholic countries, in accordance with a decree from Pope Gregory XIII, pushed their calendars ahead by ten days.

However, while moving the date up ten days solved the problem of matching the new, or Gregorian, calendar with that of the earth's, it still did nothing to fix the problem of gaining 3 days every 400 years. The Gregorian calendar solved this problem by mandating that years ending in hundreds be leap years only if divisible by 400. Confused? Well, to put it simply, in the years 1700, 1800, and 1900—normally leap years—the extra day was not added, while the year 2,000 will remain a leap year. This way, those pesky three extra days every four hundred years will be kept in check. Even more importantly for our purposes, the Gregorian calendar also established January 1 as the New Year, instead of the traditional Christian date of March 25.

It took the more conservative English until the beginning of September in 1752 to implement the Gregorian calendar. By this point in time, the Julian (or Old Style) calendar was eleven days ahead of the Gregorian (or New Style) calendar. So, when the switch was made on September 2, 1752, the following day suddenly became September 14, 1752. This change effectively made all persons born prior to this date 11 days older. If a baby was born on September 2 (according to the Old Style calendar), he or she would be twelve days old when waking up the following day, September 14 (according to the New Style calendar). It should be noted that when Parliament approved of using the Gregorian calendar, there was a great deal of public unrest, including several riots. People apparently thought that the government was pulling a fast one on them by stealing away eleven days of their lives!

Because of these changes, records having to do with the months of January, February, and March prior to 1752, will often use double dates, for example, March 18, 1675/76. This may seem confusing, but you must remember that the Old Style calendar considered January, February, and most of March to be part of the preceding year, whereas the New Style calendar made January 1 the New Year. For example, February 22, 1748 (Old Style) is the same as February 11, 1749 (New Style).

In some instances, records will explicitly refer to either the Old Style calendar or the New Style calendar, for instance, March 18, 1676 New Style (usually abbreviated N.S.). You should also be wary of records prior to 1752 which refer to the month not by name, but with a number. If a date is written as 18, 3rd month, 1675, it is most likely referring to May 18, 1675, as it is using March as the first month of the year.

Awareness of the eleven day differential and the change in the date of the New Year will help you whenever you come across certain discrepancies in birth and death records. When one record has the date of birth of an ancestor occurring eleven days earlier than another record, you can be sure that the record with the earlier date was based on the Old Style calendar. Similarly, if one record claims that an ancestor of yours gave birth to a son on April 15, 1650, and another record indicates that she also gave birth to a daughter on March 16, 1650, the latter record was most certainly using the Old Style calendar, and that the daughter was actually born on March 5, 1651.

Lastly, I would like to point out that while you may never encounter unusual dating practices in your own research, this information still provides a valuable lesson on the importance of being creative and using every available resource that is at your disposal when tracing your family roots. You must be able to keep enough of an open mind to find that *one* clue, that *one* valuable piece of information, that solves a riddle and allows you to bring your search to yet another succeeding generation instead of stopping right then and there. ALWAYS BE CURIOUS.

5

YOU AND YOUR FAMILY: YOUR MOST IMPORTANT RESOURCES

Begin with Yourself!

When beginning your search for your family roots you must commence the hunt with an examination of yourself; you are the basic building block, the foundation as it may be, of the vast sculpture that will ultimately grow to be your family tree. Besides, you are obviously the easiest subject to research!

You can start by filling out the ancestral chart as far back as you can possibly go with the knowledge you have at your immediate disposal, and then move on to your family group chart. Go as far back as you can possibly go.

You may have the urge to skip this portion of the research process, mistakenly thinking that you know it so well that you can write it all down at any time. But that is the wrong attitude to take at this point. Instead you should welcome the opportunity to get some valuable practice in research itself, recording facts and even verifying them in some cases.

One thing to be aware of, however, is the importance of obtaining accurate information at this level of your search. Any wrong information on your part at this point could lead you on an erroneous path that will take you far from where you want to be. Don't put down any information that you *think* is correct. Unless you are absolutely positive about a fact, always check it out with one or more references before assuming it to be true.

Additionally, you need to understand the importance of writing down family anecdotes, accomplishments, personality quirks . . . in general, anything that strikes you as being interesting in any way. If all you record are simple facts such as birthdays and place names, you will end up with a very dry, fairly boring family history. On the other hand, little slices of life, sad and funny tales about family members, etc., will help to make your final family history an exciting, fascinating report to read.

What to Do if You are Adopted

People who are adopted face a challenge in finding their roots which is, quite frankly, difficult to overcome. But over the past two decades there has been such an upsurge in the amount of adoptees who want to find their natural parents that it has now become a much easier task than it once was.

The first thing you should know (or perhaps already know) is that in many states adoption records are still considered private, and only an order of the court can give an adult adoptee the right to view them. Thanks to the increased interest by adoptees over the past few years, however, some states are rethinking their policy, and hopefully these records will soon be completely open. But what can you do in the interim?

There are quite a few books on the market which can give you ideas about how to conduct your search for your natural parents. Betty Jean Lifton's *Lost and Found: The Adoption Experience*, and Jayne Askin and Bob Oskam's *Search: A Handbook for Adoptees and Birth Parents* are both excellent accounts of the means by which other adult adoptees have found their birth parents. These books list in detail the organizations that can help you, as well as the states with the most open documents.

There are two agencies which can certainly be of help to you on your quest. The first is the Adoptees' Liberty Movement Association (ALMA). Members of this organization share information with each other, including any methods for gaining access to documents. They can be reached at:

ALMA
P.O. Box 154
Washington Bridge Station
New York, NY 10033

The second agency is the Orphan Train Heritage Society of America. The members of this agency were all part of an early adoption movement, known as the Orphan Train Movement, in which the Children's Aid Society of New York moved over one hundred thousand street children and orphans to loving homes in the West. This movement took place between about 1850 and 1930, and many of the children were immigrants who had lost their parents during the voyage to America or shortly after arriving. If you think you or your ancestors were part of the Orphan Train Movement, then write to:

The Orphan Train Heritage Society of America
4912 Trout Farm Rd
Springdale, AR 72764

The Next Step—Your Family Members

By beginning with live sources, you will save time, energy and just as importantly, you will have more fun! Talking with various relatives of yours will enable both of you to get to know each other better. Always remember to go as close to the source in question as possible when trying to verify facts. If this isn't possible, try to communicate with the person who is still living who was closest to the person whose facts are in question. If, for example, you wanted to find out something about your great paternal grandfather's brothers and sisters, you could go to your paternal grandfather or one of his brothers or sisters to find out the information. If your grandfather and his brothers and sisters are no longer living, you could go to

42

your father or one of your aunts or uncles. In cases involving family members with whom you are not on good terms, ask another family member who knows both of you to do the interviewing for you—but remember that this can only be considered second hand information.

Interviewing Family Members in Person

After you have contacted your relative by mail or by phone, informed them of your project and your desire to interview them, and set up a time which is *convenient for them*, there are a few guidelines to follow to make sure you get a good, fun, and factual interview. Here they are:

1) Try to conduct the interview in a one on one setting. If another relative would like to be present at the interview, by all means allow him to do so—two people talking about the past are often able to trigger memories within each other.

2) Bring a tape recorder if at all possible. Small, portable tape recorders are relatively inexpensive, and their built in microphones are unobtrusive and non-intimidating. A tape recorder will allow you to concentrate on what the person you are interviewing is saying, rather than racing to write down every word that comes out of his or her mouth. Plus, you'll have a valuable heirloom—a permanent record of an in depth conversation with your relative for succeeding generations to hear. If you have access to a video camera, you may want to consider videotaping the interview. Set the camera up on a tripod, focus in on the subject, press the record button, and begin asking your questions.

3) Prepare a list of questions on a few sheets of paper. When writing the questions, try to order them

43

in such a way so that one question leads naturally into the next. For instance, if you want to know about one relative in particular, keep all of your questions about this relative—when he was born, where he lived etc.—together, so that the interview does not jump back and forth from person to person, place to place, and decade to decade. Also, be sure to avoid questions that encourage a simple 'yes' or 'no' answer. Having trouble coming up with questions? Here are some samples to get you started. These are opening questions that might be asked of an ancestor who came to America from another country when he or she was a child: Where were you born? When did you arrive in this country? Did your family change their last name when they came to the United States? Where did your family first settle upon their arrival? What was life like during those first few years in America? Do you remember any stories about those years? What type of work did your father do? . . . .

4) LISTEN. This is the most important thing you can remember to do during an interview. Let the person you are interviewing do the talking. Never interrupt, and don't assume someone has finished just because they pause for a moment. Always wait for the person to tell you they are finished, or wait for a substantial pause before you ask your next question. If a relative seems to be wandering, talking about things you haven't asked him about, by all means let him talk. It is very likely that he'll come up with an interesting fact or insight about your roots. If he or she mentions something in passing that you would like to know more about, jot it down on a piece of paper, and when they are done talking, you can go back and ask about this fact.

5) Phrase your questions in a manner that avoids any bias on your part. For instance, instead of asking, "Your Uncle Ralph was born in New Orleans, right?" You should say, "Where was your Uncle Ralph born?"

6) Don't make the interview last too long. One or two hours should be the maximum amount of time you should impose on your subject at any one sitting. By all means, arrange for a second or even third interview if necessary, keeping in mind that two two-hour interviews are far more pleasurable and productive than one four-hour interview.

7) Treat these talks with your relatives as *conversations* rather than as a more formal interview. The more relaxed you keep the meeting, the more fun both you and the person you are interviewing will have.

8) Sometimes you may run into delicate situations involving relatives who do not care for each other, or some kind of unseemly information or even scandal that a relative does not want to discuss. These situations must be treated carefully and with a good deal of common sense. If you need to find out information about, for instance, a deceased uncle of yours, and the person you are interviewing did not like this uncle and doesn't want to discuss him, then try to find someone else who will talk about your uncle rather than pressuring someone who never got along with him. Likewise, if a relative does not want to discuss a scandalous incident in the family history, find another relative who was not connected to the scandal but who knows the details to pass on the information to you. Remember, tact and diplomacy are two important traits that you must develop and exhibit if you hope to succeed in your quest to find your family roots.

9) When it comes time to transpose the tape, don't feel as though you have to get every word your sub-

ject said down on paper. In some instances—particularly for information which you don't feel is crucial at this stage of your research—you may want to simply jot down a few words about the subject being discussed along with the point in the tape where it occurs (tape counters are especially useful for this technique).

Interviewing Family Members by Mail

Many times it is difficult to arrange a live interview with a relative because of money and/or geographical considerations. In such cases, you should try to interview your subject by mail. The first thing to do is to write up a cover letter. The following page contains an example of a good cover letter written to a relative who knows who you are.

Sample Cover Letter

Dear Aunt Violet,

As you may have heard, I have been tracing our family roots in the hopes of putting together a complete history of our family. So far it has been a tremendously exciting challenge, made much easier by all of the help I have received from my relatives, both close and distant, who have provided me with a wide variety of facts and stories.

I would be extremely grateful if you could also offer your help. I have sent along a family group chart, and I would appreciate it if you would take the time to fill it out as best you can. I have also sent along a few questions for you to answer, and would be thankful if you could answer these for me too.

When I am finished with this project, I plan on making copies for everyone in the family, and I'll be sure that you are one of the first to receive it.

Best wishes,

(your name)

PS—If you have any family records (diaries, bibles, photos, birth and death certificates, etc.) that you could possibly send me so that I may make a photocopy of them, I would be eternally grateful. Or, if you would like to make a photocopy for me, I would be more than happy to reimburse you for the cost.

Along with your cover letter, you should include a brief questionnaire, with direct, to-the-point questions. Keep the number of questions you ask to a reasonable amount, or else you might discourage your potential source (remember—you can always write again). You should also leave enough space after each question for your relative to write in his or her answer. Additionally, along with a blank family group chart, you might want to include a couple of sample charts which have already been filled out for another branch of the family. Finally, make sure you include a self-addressed, stamped envelope for their convenience.

You may also find yourself writing to a relative who you have never met, or even to someone who does not know that the two of you are related. In this instance, a cover letter that provides some background on who you are and how you are related to the person to whom you are writing will be necessary. Here is a sample opening paragraph; the remainder of the letter should be similar to the one included above:

Dear Mr. Smith:

My name is Jordan Jones, and I am your third cousin once removed. While we have never met, you may have heard about me through your grandfather, who still keeps in touch with my father (and his second cousin), Matthew Jones. You and I are related because your great-great-grandfather, Rick Jones, was the brother of my great-grandfather, Steve Jones. I realize that this can all be very confusing, so I have included a chart which will help you understand all of these intricate relationships.

I have recently become interested in tracing my family roots . . . .

Finding Relics in the Attic and Basement

When visiting or interviewing an older relative, ask if you may look at any family records he may have saved. If possible, try to gain access to attics and cellars, where things from the past have been simply packed away or discarded. I can almost guarantee that such searches will provide you with a storehouse of information. It's also a good idea to carry along a magnifying glass in order to make out old and faded handwriting. Here is what to look for:

Family Bibles—Early American tradition stipulated that the head of the family record all vital family information inside of the family bible, usually on the inside of the front cover or the first one or two pages. When checking out this information, always compare the publication date of the bible with the date of entry or date of birth of the person who recorded the information. This way, you'll be able to tell if the material was entered after the fact, or if it is indeed first hand information. You should also look carefully at the handwriting: if it is uniform throughout, then the chances are good that one person entered in the information in one sitting, from memory or second and third-hand information, long after the actual births and deaths of the parties involved; if the handwriting differs from entry to entry, and the older entries are more faded than the more recent entries, then you most likely have a much more authentic family record, as different members of the family entered in births and deaths as they actually occurred.

Diaries—While these will rarely provide you with hard core facts, they will give you a unique insight into the cultural and intellectual history of a certain period of time. It should also be noted that many diaries from colonial times have been published, and may

49

be of use to you if you are fortunate enough to trace your family roots back to the dawning of our country. Judge Samuel Sewall's *Diary* covers the Boston area from 1674 to 1729; Joshua Hempstead's diary offers a great deal of information about New London, Connecticut from 1711 to 1748; and Thomas Minor's journal covers the years 1653 to 1684 in Stonington, Connecticut.

Books—Books are a surprising fountain of information, as they often contain old letters, love notes, calling cards, newspaper clippings, and an assortment of other bits and pieces of information within their covers.

Letters—An extremely valuable source, not only for the details of your family's history which may be contained within the letters themselves, but for what's on the outside of the envelope: addresses, return addresses, postmarks, and dates.

Family Records—Wills, deeds, birth and death certificates, passports, armed forces papers, college diplomas, contracts, mortgages, church records, health papers, family account books . . . if it's a legal document of any kind, it most likely contains information that you can use.

Samplers and Quilts—If you ever come across a sampler hanging on the wall of one of your relatives, be sure to examine it closely. Often times the seamstress who created it will have included a listing of family members and their ages. If she dated the sampler, then you'll have an immediate record of the dates of birth of several members of your family! If you do discover a sampler or two in the home of one or more of your relatives, you might want to take a look at Edith Standwood Bolton's *American Samplers*, which provides a wealth of information about samplers and the data they may contain. Like the sampler, a quilt often features the names of the seamstress's friends and family, along with their dates of birth.

Miscellaneous Items—Silverware, tea pots, quilts, jewelry, watches . . . almost anything that can contain an inscription is worth taking a look at. At the very least, you should ask the relative who owns the item for an explanation, for he or she might subsequently reveal a key piece of information. You never know . . . .

6

THE TREMENDOUS
RICHES OF LIBRARIES

What You Can Find in Libraries

So you've talked or written to the living members of your family. You've talked or written to a variety of people who knew your deceased relatives. You've dug through closets and attics and cellars looking for diaries, bibles, papers, photographs . . . anything that might possibly hold a clue to your roots. "What's next?" you ask. Well, now it's time to begin writing to and visiting libraries in order to begin searching through the wealth of *published* genealogical material that is at your disposal.

Genealogical material can be found in a number of different forms. There are genealogies which have been printed and published as books; there are magazines and newspapers which publish genealogical articles and records; local histories which provide facts about the people from a particular town or area; the publications of an assortment of genealogical and historical societies; and publications by other organizations, clubs, and even universities.

The initial key to finding your way through this mass of information is to establish which line of your family you are going to search first, and in which area of the country you are going to begin your search. Armed with these basic facts, the amount of information you can find is limited only by what actually exists in print.

If you live in a metropolitan area, the chances are good that there will be a library with a solid genealogical collection in your area. But even the smallest rural library can be of great help because of the "Interlibrary Loan System." University, public, and private libraries belong to this consortium of institutions, and through it you can borrow books from libraries across the country. To make things even easier for you, the waiting period to receive books you request through the Interlibrary Loan System is usually only a week or two.

If your local library is not a member of the Interlibrary Loan System, or if your local librarian is not helpful or knowledgeable when it comes to genealogical resources, you may want to try and visit the metropolitan area closest to your home where a large genealogical collection exists, or write to librarians in other cities.

I have included a detailed state-by-state listing of libraries whose collection includes a genealogical section in the appendix of this book (see page 178).

What to Ask Librarians by Mail

Once you have established which line of your family you want to search first, and with which area of the country you will begin, you should contact a library from that region in order to obtain facts, records, or any other information which will be helpful to you as you search for your family roots.

When you write the library, there are certain guidelines you should follow:

1) You should always make the librarian's search as simple as possible. This means paying for photocopies that need to be made, sending a self-addressed-stamped envelope, and making your questions as simple and direct as possible. Don't ask rambling questions that will make the librarian do extra work. Give the full name of the person you are looking for (including any possible variants), the approximate dates of birth and death, and the name of the city and county where the person lived. And never expect the librarian to fill out any of your paperwork for you!

2) Ask about any other sources of local history the librarian can suggest. Perhaps there is a historical society in the area. Perhaps several books on local history have already been written.

3) Ask if there is already a family history on file. Perhaps someone has already compiled a genealogy, thereby saving you much labor. Don't count on this, but you should never forget to ask.

The Library of Congress

The Library of Congress is the home of the largest collection of published family histories in the United States. The tens of thousands of books are alphabetized according to family name, making it fairly simple for you to conduct your research.

If you can't visit the Library of Congress in person, you can find out if there is a published history of your family name by writing to The Library of Congress, Science and Technology Division, Washington D.C. 20540. If there is such a published history, the staff at the Library will photocopy it for you for a moderate fee.

The library puts out two very useful guides: "Out of Print Materials and Reprinted Publications" and "The Library of Congress Guide to Genealogical Research Reference Services and Facilities of the Local History and Genealogy Room" are both free of charge. These guides can answer most basic questions you have about using the facilities at the Library of Congress.

The Library of the Church of Jesus Christ of Latter-Day Saints (LDS)

As any genealogist worth a grain of salt knows, the LDS library in Salt Lake City (along with its regional branches across the United States) has the most comprehensive collection of genealogical records in the world. Every year, this church spends millions and millions of dollars on research. Why? Because their religious doctrine stipulates that all members of the church maintain a thorough and accurate record of not only their immediate family, but of their ancestors as well.

Now, you may be wondering why I am telling you this, especially if you have no affiliation with the church. Well, with upwards of 75 million records of ancestors in their vaults, there is a very good chance that the records of many of your relatives, whether or not they were in the church themselves, are contained within this massive library.

The best news, however, is that the LDS allows anyone, regardless of religious affiliation, to use their facilities. This means that all of the records of births, deaths, marriages, etc., which are contained on their microfilm files are all available for your perusal.

Obviously, the best way to utilize the LDS library is to take a trip to Salt Lake City and go through their microfilms yourself. If this is not possible for you to do, the next best thing is to visit one of the more than two hundred regional LDS libraries spread out across the United States. In such libraries, you will not find as much material as you would at the Salt Lake City branch, but you will gain access to a variety of records, and the staff at these regional libraries will be more than happy to order anything you need from the main library for a nominal charge.

The other option you have if you cannot make it to Utah is to take advantage of the LDS library's Ancestral Research Survey. For a small fee, one of the library's expert researchers will provide you with LDS records of one line of your family. You will receive a copy of your family group chart, suggestions for future research, and the names and addresses of other distant relatives of yours who are also working on putting together a Family History.

In order to get a survey done on your family, simply write to the Ancestral Research Survey, Suite 1006, 54 East South Temple Street, Salt Lake City, Utah 84111. They will send you all the necessary information. You can also go to your local branch of the LDS library and ask them for information.

Published Genealogies

To find out if the family in which you are interested has published a genealogy, your best bet is to start with one of the many indexes to printed genealogies (see the following section, "Genealogical Journals and Indexes"). These indexes will let you know if the genealogy of the family you are searching for has been published in either periodical or book form. You simply look up the name of the family—making certain you allow for variant spellings—and you will find any genealogies published on that name, including publication date, the name of the publisher, etc. Of course, there is not one index to all of the genealogies that have been published. You will have to search through whatever indexes you can get your hands on, and hopefully the name you are looking for will show up in one of these.

Once you have found a reference to a published genealogy of a family for which you are looking, you have three options: first, you can search for a copy of the genealogy in the library where you found the reference in the index; second, you can contact the publisher of the volume or a bookstore which specializes in printed genealogies to see if it is available for purchase; and third, you can contact other libraries to see if they have it in their collection.

If you are fortunate enough to find a copy of a genealogy of a family in which you are interested, and go on to discover that it indeed contains your line of descent, you can try to purchase the book from the publisher, or copy down the information and create a ancestral chart (see Chapter 3). When creating a ancestral chart, be sure to write down the page numbers where you find the information on each name you are jotting down. That way, if you ever need to go back and check a fact, you won't have to search through pages and pages to find the information.

I should mention here that just because you find a beautifully bound volume containing the genealogy of one of your lines of descent, this does not guarantee that the information is accurate. For all you know, the person who compiled the genealogy could have based it on hearsay, inaccurate memories, and the like, and then printed it and bound it in a gold-embossed leather cover to make it look extremely professional. Many times, in fact, a few scraps of faded paper can contain a genealogy that is much more accurate than one that has been printed and bound. The important lesson here is never to take any prepublished genealogy as gospel; always check dates, facts, relationships, etc., against either the original or some type of official records.

Genealogical Journals and Indexes

Genealogical journals have been published throughout the history of the United States which, of course, means that there is an overwhelming amount of published material out there to sort through. Many of these magazines publish yearly issues with information on societies and genealogical libraries. Some even invite you to write in with questions, in hopes that other readers may be able to help you out on your search for information.

Fortunately, there exists a good number of indexes to these publications, which can make locating a particular article or piece of valuable information about one of your ancestors relatively easy. Here are the names of the more informative indexes:

Barber, Gertrude A., comp. *Subject Index of the New York Genealogical and Biographical Record, Volumes 39-76 Inclusive.* New York: The Author, 1946.

Brigham, Clarence S. *History and Bibliography of American Newspapers, 1690-1820.* 2 vols. Worcester, MA: 1947.

Cappon, Lester J. *American Genealogical Periodicals: A Bibliography with a Chronological Finding-List.* New York: New York Public Library, 1962.

Columbia Library Club, comp. *The Missouri Historical Index: Volumes 1-25.* Columbia: The State Historical Society of Missouri, 1934.

Cruise, Boyd, comp. *Index to the Louisiana Historical Quarterly.* New Orleans: Plantation Bookshop, 1956.

Daughters of the American Revolution. *Genealogical Guide. Master Index of Genealogy in the DAR Magazine, vols. 184, 1892-1950.* Washington, D.C.: Daughters of the American Revolution, 1951.

Doll, Eugene E., ed. *The Pennsylvania Magazine of History and Biography: Index, Volumes 1-75.* Philadelphia: The Historical Society of Pennsylvania, 1954.

Everton, George B., ed. *The Handy Book for Genealogists.* Logan, UT: Everton Publishers, 1971.

Fisher, Carlton E. *Topical Index, Vols. 1-50, 1912-1962.* National Genealogical Society, special pub. 29. Washington, D.C.: The Society, 1964.

Genealogical Periodical Annual Index, Vols. 1-1962-. Bladensburg, MD: Ellen S. Rogers. Bowie, MD: George E. Russell.

Gerould, Winifred. American Newspapers, 1821-1936. *A Union List of Files Available in the United States and Canada.* New York: 1937.

Gregory, James P., Jr., comp. *Missouri Historical Review: Cumulative Index to Volumes 26-45.* Columbia: The State Historical Society of Missouri, 1955.

Index to the Wisconsin Magazine of History, Volumes 26-35. Madison: The State Historical Society of Wisconsin, 1955.

Jacobus, Donald L. *Index to Genealogical Periodicals.* Vol. 1, 1858-1931; vol. 2, 1932-1946; vol. 3, 1947-1952. Reprint. Baltimore: Genealogical Publishing Co., 1963-65.

Krueger, Lillian, comp. *The Wisconsin Magazine of History: Index, Volumes 1-15.* Madison: The State Historical Society of Wisconsin, 1934.

Parsons, Margaret Wellington, ed. *Index (Abridged) to the New England Historical and Genealogical Register: Volumes 51 through 112.* Marlborough, MA: The Author, 1959.

Riker, Dorothy, comp. *Indiana Magazine of History: General Index, Volumes 1-25.* 1930. Reprint. New York: Kraus Reprint Corp., 1967.

Royne, Josephine E., and Chapman, Effie L., eds. *New England Historical and Genealogical Register: Index of Persons, Subjects, Places, Vols. 1-50.* 3 vols. 1906-1911. Reprint. Baltimore: GPC, 1972.

Russell, George E. *Genealogical Periodicals Annual Index.* Vol. 5-, 1966-. Bowie, MD: The Author, 1967-.

Spear, Dorothea N. *Bibliography of American Directories through 1860*. Worcester, MA: American Antiquarian Society, 1961.

Supplement to Genealogical Guide: Master Index of Genealogy in the DAR Magazine, Vols. 85-89, 1950-1955. Washington, D.C.: Daughters of the American Revolution, 1956.

Swem, E.G., comp. *Virginia Historical Index*. Gloucester, MA: Peter Smith, 1965.

Waldenmaier, Inez. *Annual Index to Genealogical Periodicals and Family Histories*. Vols. for 1956-1962. Washington, D.C.

Youngs, Florence E. *Subject Index of the New York Genealogical & Biographical Record, Vols. 1-38*. New York, 1907.

Genealogical Book Sellers

Whether you locate a particular publication in one of the indexes mentioned above, or if you simply want to inquire about published material on a certain region of the country, the genealogical publishers and book sellers listed on the following pages should be able to help you. Write to them requesting either their catalog (usually free) or information on a particular publication in which you are interested.

East
Carl-Del-Scribe
Box 746
Burlington, VT 05401

Connecticut Society
of Genealogists, Inc.
Box 305
West Hartford, CT 06107

Fortunate Finds Bookstore
16 West Natick Road
Warwick, RI 02886

Goodspeed's Book Shop, Inc.
7 Beacon Street
Boston, MA 02108

Genealogist's Bookshelf
Box 468, 330 East 85th Street
New York, NY 10028

Hoenstine Book Mart
Box 208
Holidaysburg, PA 16648

George S. MacManus
Company
2022 Walnut Street
Philadelphia, PA 19103

New England Historic
and Genealogical Society
101 Newbury Street
Boston, MA 02116

New York Public Library
Grand Central Station, Box 2747
New York, NY 10017

Tuttle Antiquarian Books, Inc.
28 South Main Street
Rutland, VT 05701

South
American Association
for State and Local History
132 9th Ave. North
Nashville, TN 37208

Appalachia Book Shop
1316 Pen Mar Ave.
Bluefield, WV 24701

Book Shelf
3765 Hillsdale Drive, N.E.
Cleveland, TN 37311

Genealogical Book Company
521-23 St. Paul's Place
Baltimore, MD 21202

Holmes-Corey Antiquities
Box 115M
Marco Island, FL 33937

Kentucky Publishing
Company
153 Cherokee Park
Lexington, KY 40503

Magna Carta Book Company
5324 Beaufort Ave.
Baltimore, MD 21215

Polyanthos, Inc.
822 Orleans St.
New Orleans, LA 70116

Reprint Company
154 W. Cleveland Park Dr.
Spartanburg, SC 29303

Southern Historical Press
Box 229
Easley, SC 29640

Walton-Folk Americana
330 Cherokee Street
Kennesaw, GA 30144

Wolf's Head Books
P.O. Box 1048
198 Foundry St.
Morgantown, WV 26507

Midwest
Bland Books
401 N.W. 10th Street
Fairfield, IL 62837

The Bookmark
Box 74
Knightstown, IN 46148

Gale Research Company
Book Tower
Detroit, MI 48226

Heritage Resource Center
Box 26305
Minneapolis, MN 55426

Hoosier Heritage Press
520 N. Campbell Street
Indianapolis, IN 46219

West
Albaltoss Book Store
166 Eddy Street
San Francisco, CA 94102

Ancient Book Shop
Box 986
Santa Fe, NM

The Augustan Society
Hartwell Company
1617 West 261st Street
Harbor City, CA 90710

Brigham Young
University Press
205 University Press Bldg.
Provo, UT 84602

Clark's Old Book Store
318 West Sprague
Spokane, WA 99204

Dawson Book Shop
550 S. Figueroa Street
Los Angeles, CA 90017

Deseret Book Company
44 East South Temple
Salt Lake City, UT 84110

Everton Publishers, Inc.
Box 368
Logan, UT 84321

Hawkes Publishing, Inc.
156 West 2170 South
Salt Lake City, UT 84115

Heritage Research Institute
964 Laird Avenue
Salt Lake City, UT 84105
(Origins of names)

Saddleback Book Shop
Box 10393
Santa Ana, CA 92771

San Francisco
Historical Records
1204 Nimitz Dr.
Colma, CA 94015

Wahrenbroch's Book House
726 Broadway
San Diego, CA 92101

Local Histories

With a little research, you will discover that most towns and cities have published local histories about their foundings and important historical events. You should certainly look through the history books of the area where your ancestor lived. If he was a noted member of the community, then the local history might even contain an accurate genealogy of your family! If, however, no such genealogy is printed in the local history, then you should not give up hope. These books are filled with tremendous amounts of useful information. For example, you can find out where the founders of the town came from, which might point you to a new area in which to continue your search.

The best index of local histories currently available is called the *United States Local Histories in the Library of Congress: A Bibliography*. Regrettably, this listing is far from complete, and you will probably have to do some more extensive research in the genealogical societies and libraries of the state in which your ancestor lived in order to find all its local histories. But don't despair; since genealogical librarians are aware of the need for an informative index, they are often well versed in the local histories of their state and can be very helpful in your search.

Newspapers

Newspapers have existed since before the United States was an independent country. While searching through microfilms of newspapers can be quite a chore, the proliferation of newspaper indexes within the last few years has made this research process much less time consuming.

The most obvious information contained in newspapers that is useful to the genealogist are marriage and birth notices, and obituaries. However, papers such as the *Boston Evening Transcript* and the *Hartford Times* once published a genealogical column aimed specifically at people who were searching for lost relatives and information on ancestors who have long since passed away. While neither paper still runs these columns, the information is still readily available. Check with your local library, or visit or write to the Library of Congress and ask for information on newspaper indexes and how best to utilize them. Incidentally, Rider's *American Genealogical-Biographical Index* lists every name found in the *Boston Evening Transcript's* column from 1906 to 1941.

Genealogical and Historical Societies

By joining a genealogical or historical society, you gain access to magazines, books, libraries . . . a host of genealogical information that can only save you time and money, while providing you with facts you may have never thought would be possible to discover. The Genealogy Club of America is an excellent society for the beginning genealogist to join, as they tend to take a more serious view of people who are simply interested in tracing their family roots as opposed to other societies who are primarily concerned with professional genealogists.

In the appendix of this book (see page 197), you will find a state-by-state list of the names and addresses of genealogical and historical societies. Since the membership rules (some require no membership at all in order to use their facilities, while others are more rigid) and resource materials vary from organization to organization, I suggest you begin with those societies closest to your home or the home of the ancestor you are most interested in researching.

Schools, Colleges, and Fraternity Records

Educational files often contain a great deal of biographical data which can be of immense use to the genealogist. If you know precisely where your ancestor lived, you can comb through local records to find out which schools were in existence at that time and then try to seek out the records of these schools. Beginning with the private school of your ancestor's religious affiliation may save you time, since this was how many private schools operated before the existence of a public school system.

If you think that your ancestor may have attended college, you might want to check with some of the older universities around the country, including: William Penn in Philadelphia, Boston Latin School, Harvard, William and Mary, Roxbury Latin School in Roxbury, Massachusetts, and Yale. These institutions of higher education have enrollment records, yearbooks, rosters, and student files reaching all the way back to their founding years.

Finally, contacting the National Intrafraternity Conference through a local university may ultimately lead you to a great deal of biographical information on one of your ancestors if, of course, he was a member of a fraternity at one time or another.

Private Clubs

One important type of miscellaneous record that you should not overlook are those kept by the private clubs which have existed in this country for decades and decades. The Elks, Masons, Knights of Columbus, and the Rotary, Kiwanis, and Lions clubs have files on their members dating back to the founders of the association. Such records contain highly detailed biographical information and occasionally even photographs of the member. You should contact the local president of the club—either in your or your ancestor's home town—to which you believe your ancestor may have belonged in order to find out how you can receive a copy of your ancestor's file.

Perhaps the most important information that can be gleaned from such clubs and organizations is a notion of your ancestor's hobbies and interests. Imagine how exciting and *alive* your family album can be if you include such details from the past!

7

CHURCH RECORDS
AND CEMETERIES

Keepers of the Records
of Western Civilization

The Church is one of the oldest organized institutions in Western civilization. Prior to the Reformation in Europe, such members of the clergy as monks and priests were the only people who could read and write (this was necessary for them to study their religious verse). As such, the duty to keep state records naturally fell to them, as kings were anxious to have accurate records of the citizenry so that no one could escape the burden of taxes.

The repercussions of this are astonishing. In theory, fairly accurate records have been kept by various religious organizations for almost a thousand years! Church records are, therefore, a gold-mine of information for a genealogist such as yourself, allowing you to trace your roots farther back than you ever dreamed possible.

But if you're thinking all of this just seems *too* good to be true, then I have to admit that you are right. Church records have been kept for almost a thousand years, but in many cases their accuracy is in question. In Europe, where the church and the state have traditionally acted as one body, corruption undoubtedly tainted the records. In America, where the church has always been forced away from state affairs, meticulous record-keeping was not seen as a duty of the clergy. More to the point, innumerable records have been destroyed by natural disaster and warfare. Can you imagine how many records were lost in Europe due to the bombing raids of World War II?

But don't lose heart. Even though many of these church records were lost, many more still exist today. Some contain information that cannot be found anywhere else, and some contain facts which can corroborate information found in other records. In other words, if you are willing to analyze church records closely, comparing them with other documents whenever possible, then they can still provide you with a wealth of knowledge about your past!

Church records can be a secret weapon to utilize if you are having trouble locating the birth, marriage, and/or death certificates of a particular ancestor of yours. These records do vary among the different denominations: Quaker churches traditionally maintained highly meticulous logs, recording the marriage, birth, and death of a church member; Baptist, United Brethren, and other religions spawned in America recorded membership rosters, but almost never logged births, christenings, deaths, or marriages; Dutch Reformed, Anglican, Catholic, and other European religions usually maintained histories of births, christenings, marriages, deaths, and burials.

How to Use Church Records

In order to use church records effectively, it is vital that you remember two important trends in American religious history. Firstly, when Europeans initially came to this continent and formed the colonies, they were so distrustful of the church entering into their affairs that religious wedding ceremonies were outlawed. Weddings were considered entirely civil affairs, and as a result they were performed by civil magistrates. Therefore, if you find mention of a wedding in an extremely old church record (one that dates back to the colonies), then take a closer look at it; the record is probably not of a wedding but of a marriage bann, or an intention to marry, and there is no guarantee that such a marriage ever took place. If you assume that such a bann was fulfilled, then you might start

71

researching the wrong family by mistake. The second trend you should be aware of is that religious groups in America have traditionally gone out and proselytized new members—we've all heard of the famous preachers who traveled the Old West, for example. As a result, names simply appear and disappear from church records, indicating that a person or family converted to a different faith.

What should you do if the name you are tracing suddenly disappears from a church record? How can you possibly guess to which religion your ancestor had previously belonged? This is actually quite simple. If you are aware of the European homeland of your ancestors, which most of us are, then you can figure out your family's original religion. If they were German or Dutch, then chances are they were either Dutch Reformed, Lutheran, or Catholic. If they were from Italy, then there is a good chance they were Catholic. And if they were from Scotland or Ireland, they were probably Presbyterian. Knowing this, you can then narrow down in which colony they settled. Catholics usually made homes for themselves in Maryland. Presbyterians usually lived in Virginia. And Pennsylvania was populated by practitioners of just about every religion.

Here is an example of how to use this information. Say you have managed to trace your ancestor back to the Old West, and you have found his name in a United Brethren church record. But there is no listing of his parents in any membership roster, suggesting that he converted his faith when he became a pioneer and moved out West. You are aware, however, that your family originally came to America from Scotland, which means they were probably Presbyterian. Therefore, if you scour the Presbyterian records

72

of Virginia, you will probably find your ancestor's name in their books. Now you not only have documents recording his life, but you've also learned about the exciting journey he made across the country!

The single biggest problem with church records from this country is that they are rarely complete. Ministers and priests usually had to maintain records by themselves, and they were notoriously bad at doing so. This is somewhat understandable, when you remember that they frequently moved from one area to the next, and that frontier towns rarely had any records at all! Can you imagine a preacher riding through the Old West actually taking the time to log the names of his converts? Even worse, when a priest actually did keep accurate records, he sometimes took them with him when he moved, instead of leaving them for his successor. Moreover, it was practically impossible for a conscientious priest to keep thorough records at all, because they were so easily destroyed by the harsh conditions of life in America.

But do not despair! Be glad that church records exist at all, as they can be such a wonderful source of information. You should never forget to check for the existence of church records about your ancestors; if available, they can provide you with at least as much information as government records. But they can also tell you about the intangible qualities of the lives of your ancestors: if they were devout churchgoers; if they were firmly established in the community; what their life was like, etc.

The Diaries of Ministers and Priests

Perhaps the best (and most difficult to find) church records are the private record diaries of ministers and priests. As these were personal documents of the oc-

73

currences at a certain church, they are much more likely to be complete and accurate than official records. Wouldn't you rather write in a diary than go through the drudgery of filling out paperwork? Regrettably, you cannot count on the existence of such books, but never forget to inquire about them when searching through the documents in a church.

Baptismal Records

When reading church records, keep in mind that if only one parent was a member of a particular church, then only his or her name may be listed on membership rosters. This is also true for the children of a married couple, who do not always join the same church as their parents, and thus would not be included on their parents' church records. The easiest way to determine how many members of the family attended the same church is to find the baptismal records of a child; such records will most likely list the names of the parents present at the ceremony. If only one parent was present, then the other probably did not belong to the same church. If, however, you find the baptismal records for several children, and sometimes both parents are listed as attending and sometimes only one, then this indicates that both parents were members of the same church, but one was simply not able to attend all the ceremonies.

When going through the baptismal records for a family with several children, you might notice a change in one of the parents' names. This means that, regrettably, one of the parents died from the hardships of life in early America, and the other remarried shortly thereafter. If one has died, then it will most likely be the mother, as child birth was a leading cause of death at the time. It is vital that you correctly note the names of the parents of the ancestor you are researching; if, for example, you fail to notice a change in the name of the father between the first and the second children, then you will start tracing the wrong family line.

Records of Admittance

Another important church document is called the record of admittance. Whenever a family moved to a new town, they had to join one of the local churches in order to become true members of the community. These records not only specifically state which members of the family joined a particular church, but they also often give clues as to which church (and in which town) the family used to belong to, allowing you to trace your ancestors back to different areas. Records of admittance can also help clarify any confusion surrounding conversions to different religions; if a person decided to change his faith, then a priest would often make a record of his admittance into the new church.

Let me give you an example in order to help you understand the information above. Suppose you are tracing an ancestor named Karl Becker, Jr. This is obviously a German name (see Chapter 4), indicating that the family was probably initially either Dutch Reformed, Lutheran, or Catholic, and that the first generation to come to America probably settled in Pennsylvania. You have found a baptismal record for Karl Becker, Jr., in a United Brethren church in the Midwest. This record also indicates that Karl had an older brother, Franck, and that the two boys had different mothers. Franck's mother was Gretta, and Karl's mother was Marie; you have no blood relation to Gretta, as she must have died prior to Karl's birth.

The baptismal records list a man named Karl Becker as the father of both Franck and Karl, Jr. You also find records of admission for Karl Becker (Karl, Jr.'s father) and Gretta Becker, but none for Marie. This means that the United Brethren priest kept sloppy records, and did not bother to properly record Marie's admission to the church when she married Karl. The record of admission notes that Karl and Gretta came from Pennsylvania. Upon researching various documents in Pennsylvania churches, you deduce that the family was originally Lutheran. You see, it's not so difficult after all!

How to Obtain Church Records

In order to obtain the record from a church which is still in operation, you can either visit the church directly, or write to the pastor of the church. If the church records you are searching for are from a church which no longer exists, the best thing to do is to write either to a local historical society or to the archives of the particular denomination in which you are interested. If they do not possess the records in question, then they can probably suggest who does. Here are some address of churches which keep archives (there are many others, not to mention several Jewish archives, which are listed in the section on Jewish Roots in the country-by-country listings in Chapter 10):

American Baptist Historical Society
1106 South Goodman Street
Rochester, NY 14620

American Congregational Association
Congregational Library
14 Beacon Street
Boston, MA 02108

American Catholic Historical Association
Catholic University of America
Washington, D.C. 20017

Archives of the Greek Orthodox
Arch-Diocese of North America
10 East 79th Street
New York, NY 10021

Archives of the Mother Church
The First Church of Christ Scientist
107 Falmouth Street
Boston, MA 02110

Church of Jesus Christ of Latter-Day Saints
Genealogical Association
54 East South Temple Street, Suite 1006
Salt Lake City, UT 84111

Chicago Theological Seminary Hammond Library
5757 South University Avenue
Chicago, IL 60637

Congregational Christian Historical Society
14 Beacon Street
Boston, MA 02108

Lutheran Ministerium of Pennsylvania
Historical Society
Lutheran Theological Seminary
7333 Germantown Avenue
Philadelphia, Pennsylvania 19119

Mennonite Historical Library
Bluffton College
Bluffton, OH 45817

77

Moravian Archives
North Main at Elizabeth
Bethlehem, Pennsylvania 18015

Presbyterian & Reformed Church
Historical Foundation
Assembly Drive
Montreat, NC 28757

Princeton Theological Seminary Speer Library
Mercer Street and Library Place
Box 111
Princeton, NJ 08542

The Protestant Episcopal Church
Church Historical Society
606 Rathervue Place
Austin, TX 78700

Union Theological Seminary Burke Library
3041 Broadway at Reinhold Niebuhr Place
New York, NY 10027

Yale University Divinity School Library
409 Prospect Street
New Haven, CT 06520

Clearly, if you are not careful when researching church records, you can easily get lost in a muddle of paperwork. It is therefore advisable for you to do a bit of reading on the subject beforehand, in order to familiarize yourself with the area. *A Survey of American Church Records*, by E. Kay Kirkham, is an extremely useful church directory. *Records of the Roman Catholic Church in the United States as a Source for Authentic Ge-*

nealogical and Historical Material is also very helpful if you are of Catholic descent. If your ancestor was a Quaker, then I highly recommend the *Encyclopedia of American Quaker Genealogy*.

Cemeteries—Genealogies Written in Stone

At the turn of the century, when the industrial revolution had been completed in America, a massive change took place: the country became more democratic. Thanks to machinery, the ability to mass produce goods and reap crops fell into the hands of the many, forever shifting the economic balance of the country. The aristocratic existence of a few, favored families came to a grinding halt as entrepreneurial-minded men and women made the country what it is today. While this process of democratization was clearly a good thing, it does pose a problem for the genealogist.

The revolution was so profound that it actually cast a rather contemptuous shadow over the 19th century, and as a result many of the cemeteries and grave sights of that period have been destroyed through neglect or willful action. Even more to the point, a beautiful part of the cultural heritage of this country has been essentially erased from the memories of this nation's children.

As a genealogist, one of your duties will be to overcome this situation. How can you do that? The answer is very simple: by caring!

Cemeteries, as you will soon understand, are one of the most important tools of the genealogist, allowing you to make connections in family trees and fill in gaps that plague your work sheets. When you begin your search for your roots, you will discover very quickly how much you care about graveyards; you will begin to think of a graveyard as a genealogy written in stone, rather than on paper. You will look at visiting them as a way of remembering and celebrating your past, and you will actually begin to *enjoy* them! After all, cemeteries commemorate those who have touched and shaped our lives.

Many genealogists and genealogical societies across the country have undergone campaigns to restore cemeteries to their former glory. I truly urge you to follow their lead, as you will be preserving the American heritage for future generations to enjoy. And now I will explain exactly why cemeteries are so important to *you*!

If you are having trouble finding records regarding the birth or death of one of your ancestors, your next step should definitely be to visit the graveyard where your ancestor is buried. To locate the cemetery in which your ancestor is buried, contact a local historical society in the town in which your ancestor died, or simply contact local cemeteries in the town and county where you think your ancestor may be buried. If you are certain that your ancestor lived and died in a particular town, but you cannot find his grave in any of the cemeteries, then check all of the graveyards in nearby towns, as borders may have moved. Don't forget to look into the possibility of private graveyards, which is particularly likely if your ancestor owned a large estate or farm. Whenever possible, take an older relative with you to the cemetery, as he or she may have visited the grave before and perhaps knows of other ancestors buried close by.

If you are unable to find your ancestor's grave in a public cemetery, then the first person you should try to speak with is a sexton. A sexton is essentially the financial operator of a cemetery, and as such he presides over meticulous financial records that date back many years. You should visit all the sextons in the town in which your ancestor lived and ask to go through their records; you might find that your ancestor did indeed buy a plot in a particular cemetery, but that the gravestone has now simply deteriorated from exposure to the elements. The sexton's records not only mention who is buried, but also indicate who actually bought the plot (and when they did it), and sometimes even where the deceased came from and his cause of death.

How to Record Information from a Tombstone

A tremendous amount of information on your ancestor can be gleaned simply from reading the tombstone. The most obvious information is his full name, date of birth, and date of death. But you can also find out much more. If he is buried in a family plot with his parents and siblings, then this indicates that he probably never got married; moreover, it also indicates that his siblings probably never married. If the dates of death for most people in the family plot are very similar, then you can be quite certain that the town was ravaged by a disease (you may want to check some other tombstones to confirm this). A local history might even mention that such a disease hit the town. But just because your ancestor is buried with his parents, don't jump to the conclusion that he was never married. Perhaps he was married, but he died while his wife was still young enough to remarry; she is probably buried with her second husband. Clearly, a wealth of knowledge can be gained by simply visiting a cemetery and seeing with whom your ancestor is buried. You can also find out a great deal about the

81

town in which your ancestor lived and the nature of life there, as in the case with the disease.

If the ancestor you are tracing is a woman, then you may be able to discover her maiden name through gravestones; married couples were *sometimes* buried in the wife's family plot. If, for example, you are tracing Jane Doe, and you find John and Jane Doe surrounded by tombstones all sharing the name Smith, then Jane's maiden name might have been Smith. This is not a very accurate way of determining maiden names, however, so you should make every effort to find documents which include them.

Reading inscriptions on gravestones is an art unto itself. As I mentioned earlier, many of them have deteriorated so much that they are extremely difficult to read. In addition, many inscriptions are written in archaic or foreign languages, and quite often they are carved in an elaborate font that makes it difficult to distinguish one letter from another. Tombstones are also made out of varying grades of stone, some of which were extremely soft and vulnerable; as a result, the writing on these stones may be particularly illegible. A good rule to go by is that if you cannot properly read a name or number, don't assume anything, because you might be dead wrong.

Rather than simply write down the inscription in a note book, I suggest you do three things. First, you should bring along a shovel, a small pair of shears, a wire brush, and some chalk. After clearing away and cleaning up the area around the headstone and the stone itself, rub the piece of chalk over the gravestone so that the lettering is easier to read. Second, take a photograph of the tombstone. Third, make a rubbing of the headstone. Place a piece of wax paper over the tombstone, and rub the paper with crayon or soft pencil; this might reveal some information that you were not able to see with your eye due to poor lighting (that number that you could have sworn was a 1 might actually turn out to be a 7). If possible, I suggest that you ask one of the cemetery workers to help you read the stone, as they have a great deal of experience in doing so.

After completing these tasks, you should then write down the information in your records. Copy it down exactly as it is written, never changing any of the wording. For example, if the stone reads "Jane Doe, consort of John Doe," don't replace the word consort with wife. Consort means that her husband was alive at the time of her death, but wife can mean that he was either dead or alive. Your accuracy is especially vital if you need a translation of the inscription.

If you still cannot read every word of the inscription when you write the information down in your records, write down any words (or portions of words) that are in question inside brackets. For example, "[Jan]e Doe." This way you can be sure to remember which part was taken from the stone, and which part you deduced through other information.

It is ironic that cemeteries, the homes of the deceased, bring the past back to life so vibrantly. They are an invaluable tool to you, and no genealogical search can ever be complete without them.

8

LOCAL AND STATE RECORDS

Primary Sources

In the world of researching, there are basically two types of sources: primary and secondary. Secondary sources contain information that is not officially recorded, but is rather reported via a secondhand source. Two examples of this are stories from relatives and entries in a family bible.

Primary sources of information, or official records and documents, are usually far more accurate, and therefore valuable, to the genealogist. The most important examples of primary sources that I have introduced so far are church records. As you now know, these documents are often quite reliable, and they are also official records, as opposed to the bible entries mentioned above.

There is one incredible advantage to using primary sources of information: such records not only give you the information you are seeking (such as a birth date), but they almost always provide you with additional information. For example, a birth certificate from a church will not only mention the date of birth of a particular ancestor, but it will also indicate the name of that ancestor's parents. As a result you should always make every attempt to locate and use primary sources before resorting to secondary ones.

The next source of primary information I want to discuss are local and state records. These documents can be categorized into two sections: criminal and civil. Criminal records are self explanatory, and will most likely not be used by you during your search. Civil records, on the other hand, are the genealogist's gold mine. Civil records are divided into three categories: vital, probate, and land records. Along with providing you with information you have not been able to discover throughout the early portion of your search, these records will enable you to verify any facts you feel may be suspect.

Generally, most of the primary records you will be searching for are located in the courthouses of the individual towns and counties in which your ancestor lived; in many parts of the northeast, however, they are often filed in the State Archival Depository of the state in which your ancestor lived. The person who is responsible for supervising such records is known as the "clerk of the court" or the "recorder of deeds."

Two Methods of Researching Primary Source Records

There are two methods you can use in your search for primary source records: searching by mail and searching in person. Each has its own advantages and disadvantages, as I will explain below.

The advantage to conducting your search through the mail is that of cost; your ancestors may have traveled far and wide, and it could become quite expensive if you try to visit courthouses across the country in person. But the disadvantages to this method are extreme. Firstly, you are not alone in your desire to conduct a genealogical search, and as a result clerks of the court receive a constant deluge of requests like yours. Clerks try to be as helpful as they can, but sometimes it is impossible for them to respond to your inquiry. Moreover, if you do not personally inspect the many records available at a courthouse, then you have no chance of stumbling across any missing links in your family group charts.

If you do opt to write to a clerk of the court, the following hints will increase your chances of receiving a helpful response:

1. Keep your letter brief and make the search as easy as possible for the clerk. Always include a self-addressed, stamped envelope for the response, and offer to pay for any costs incurred by the clerk's search.

2. Be specific. Give the exact name of the ancestor for whom you are searching (including any variant spellings), the exact type of record you need, and an estimate of the date when the record was filed. For example, if you are looking for the marriage certificate of a man who was born around 1830, then ask them to look in the records dated around 1850 (since most people used to get married in their late teens to early twenties).

3. If possible, ask for a photocopy of the document. Otherwise, ask that any and all pertinent information included in the record, such as dates and witnesses, be supplied.

The second method, that of going to various court-houses in person, has the disadvantage of being fairly expensive. This is especially true if you accidentally visit one that has no records of your ancestor. It is, however, the only way to ensure an accurate, heart-felt search. As mentioned before, you might inadvertently stumble across information, such as the names of other relatives who lived in the area, that can fill in gaps in your genealogy; there is no way that a clerk is going to perform a thorough enough search to fill in such gaps, especially if it requires looking for different surnames.

Where to Begin

Your first step will be to figure out when and where the particular ancestor you are researching did something that would cause him to be entered into the official records. This action could be something as significant as a birth, death, or marriage, or something more trivial like a land purchase.

After collecting all of the information already suggested in this book (everything from local histories to church records), you should have some idea of where your ancestor lived. You will also have a general notion of the migratory patterns of your ancestors, allowing you to figure out if an area was home to just one generation, or if many generations lived there. If several generations lived in one town or county, then one or two courthouses might have a great deal of the information you need for your genealogy; but if you want to receive all this information through the mail, then don't expect the clerk to search for it all at once.

The Surname Index

As with church records, the volume of local and state records is astounding. It would be impossible for one person to search through all of the thousands of record books in even a single courthouse. That is why most courthouses have an index known as the surname index. This index will direct you to any books containing records with your ancestor's surname. Each book, in turn, is ordered by date, further simplifying your search. If, for example, you want to find the birth certificate of an ancestor named Becker, and you know he was born sometime between 1860 and 1875, then simply search through the ten or twenty books which include the name Becker and cover that fifteen year period.

Sometimes, regrettably, you will come across a courthouse that does not have a surname index. In this case, each record book will usually have an index within its pages. This is not as convenient as a surname index, as it requires you to look through the indexes of every record book covering a certain period. In the example above, if a surname index is not available, then you would most likely have to look through the indexes of fifty to one hundred books. Although flipping through indexes of names does not take much time at all (they will always be in alphabetical order), this system is clearly not as convenient as the surname index.

Official Court Records: Criminal and Civil

I have already mentioned that court records can be either criminal or civil, and that you will most likely concern yourself with the civil ones. Many genealogists, even ones with much more experience than you, quake at the thought of going through the mass of these court records, but I cannot urge you strongly enough to take the time to do so. They often contain information that cannot be found elsewhere, and different types of civil documents can tell you about various aspects of your ancestor's life.

Within the three subdivisions of civil records (vital, probate, and land) you will find many types of documents. These include dockets, orders of the court, registers of action, birth certificates, marriage licenses and records, leases, deeds, wills, and a host of others.

Vital Documents

Vital documents are those which record the birth, death, and/or marriage of an individual. Such documents have been kept with varying degrees of accuracy since the first towns were formed in the United States, but they were not required by federal law until as late as the beginning of this century! As a result, records for a person who either was born or died in the twentieth century are fairly easy to find—simply write to the proper state office of vital records. A state-by-state list has been included in the appendix of this book to help you in your search for vital documents (see page 217).

For records which pre-date the twentieth century, you may have to do some digging, but you will probably come up with the information you need. The areas with the most inaccuracies and omissions of these documents are, naturally, pioneer towns and frontier lands.

A wonderful guide is available from the federal government which can point you in the right direction in your search for birth and death records. It tells you where you can find such information in each state and how much it will cost you to obtain it. The only drawback is that it only shows you how to find documents that were recorded after approximately the year 1900. The guide, which is free, is called *Where to Write for Birth and Death Certificates*. You can get a copy by writing to:

The U.S. Government Printing Office
Superintendent of Documents
Washington, D.C. 20402

In order to find the birth and death certificates of ancestors before the twentieth century, you will have to contact the local courthouses by one of the three methods mentioned earlier.

You may remember from the previous chapter that marriages were considered entirely civil affairs early in the history of this country. As a result, there is a wealth of civil documents available about marriages (and divorces) that dates back to the colonial period. Marriage records were not standardized until recently (there are, in fact, still several states which defy standardization by not demanding blood tests), so you might find these documents referred to as applications, bonds, certificates, consents, intentions, licenses, registers, etc. Some of these are records of the marriage itself, while others are merely civil versions of banns, so read each document very carefully. These records are available at local courthouses.

The federal government also puts out two guides about marriage and divorce records, both of which are available to you at no cost. Both deal with documents recorded since the beginning of this century. In order to receive either *Where to Write For Marriage Records* or *Where to Write for Divorce Records*, write to the U.S. Government Printing Office at the above address.

Probate Records: Wills and Testaments

Many genealogists consider probate records to be the most important documents available to them. The chief form of probate records (also known as estate records) are wills and testaments. When dealing with probate records, you will probably come across a tremendous amount of legal jargon that you are unfamiliar with, and as a result I highly recommend that you invest in a dictionary of legal terms. You might even find it useful to consult your lawyer at one point or another in order to interpret certain records, but remember that you will probably be charged a fee for such a service. Probate records can usually be found in local courthouses. The index in which they are listed is usually named "The Index to Administrations and Estates."

Wills and testaments have existed since the dawn of civilization, and examples of them have been found in many ancient cultures. Technically, the testament is concerned with the disposal of land, while the will primarily deals with an individual's personal property. During your search you are likely to come across both written and oral (nuncupative) wills and testaments. Oral ones were more common in earlier centuries, when many people did not know how to write, and writing utensils were not always readily available. Both are valid.

When an individual dies, the probate court appoints an executor to his will. The executor delivers the will to the court and proves its validity through the testimony of witnesses who were present at its signing (or present to hear it stated, in the case of oral wills). If the court rules that the will is valid, then it is declared *testate*, and the executor is ordered to distribute the land and possessions accordingly. If it is ruled invalid, then the court declares it *intestate*, in which case an administrator is appointed to dispose of all lands and properties. Such action usually results when a will fails to take into account an individual's debts. If no will is left whatsoever, then the court immediately rules that the individual died *intestate*.

Incidentally, married women did not have the right to a will until quite recently, as the court viewed their property as belonging to the husband. If the husband died and left the woman a widow, however, she then gained the right to a will, unless she remarried.

The reason that wills and testaments are so valuable to genealogists is that they are the single best indications of relationships that are available. An individual usually bequeaths land and property to his wife, to his children (from oldest to youngest), and sometimes to distant relatives such as grandchildren. Even when a will is declared *intestate*, the administrator must still make a record of the individual's relations. By now you should be aware to always be on the lookout for clerical errors in documents, and wills and testaments are no exception to this rule, but they are usually so precise that genealogists often consider them more accurate than censuses dating earlier than the mid-nineteenth century!

Much like religious documents, wills allow you to peek into the lives of your ancestors. You might find accurate inventories of your ancestor's possessions, allowing you to determine his or her standard of living and social rank in the community. You can find the exact plots of land your ancestor owned, and perhaps even arrange to visit them. You can determine whom your ancestor loved and whom he hated—did he specifically exclude someone from the will? The extent you can learn from a will is quite astounding.

When writing to a county clerk requesting a copy of a last will and testament, you might find that you can only receive an "abstraction," or parts of the document, rather than the whole will itself. In such cases, be sure to ask for the following information:

1) The name of the person who's will it is, the cause of his death, and the place he was living at the time of his death.

2) The name of every person mentioned in the will and their relationship to the deceased.

3) A list of the property that was bequeathed.

4) The names of all witnesses and executors.

5) A description of any other useful information contained within the document itself, including seals and signatures.

But wills are not the only valuable probate records. You will find many others, including accounts and settlements, petitions, sales, returns, and bonds. Three of the more valuable estate records are the appointment of guardianship, the record of distribution, and the record of lawsuits.

Appointment of guardianship can give you a good idea of the condition of your ancestor's marriage. If a man died, his wife did not necessarily become the guardian of their children. If, for example, a record indicates that the man wished his sister in another state to be the guardian, then you can probably assume that his marriage was not very stable. Sometimes appointments of guardianship were even made for handicapped or elderly people. It was not uncommon for any of these appointments to be challenged, so the documents you find may indicate that you have to do further research outside of probate records.

The record of distribution is an addendum to a will that not only lists the recipients and their relationship to the deceased, but it also indicates how the estate was divided up proportionately. If any particular relative received a disproportionate amount of the estate, then this might be an indication that he or she was particularly close to the deceased. If an individual died without creating a will, then the record of distribution might be your only way of determining relationships and divisions of property and land.

Finally, while records of lawsuits are usually not teeming with genealogical information, they can often give you an idea of family relationships. Wills and testaments were often disputed by relatives who felt they had been cheated out of an inheritance, and such documents can bring to life the attitudes your ancestors felt toward each other. Whenever possible, I recommend examining these records, as they will undoubtedly make your genealogy more fun and exciting. A genealogy, after all, is not a list of names, but rather a permanent *memory* of the lives of your ancestors.

Land Records

Land records include deeds, leases, mortgages, contracts . . . basically anything that has to do with the buying and selling of land. The most important type of land record for your purposes is the "multiple-grantor deed," which lists all sales of a deceased landowner's property by his children. This document will include the names and birthdays of both the children and their spouses, from the oldest to the youngest child in the family.

When checking out land deeds, look to see how the owner of the property acquired the piece of land, since there is a good possibility that he received it from an ancestor, which will provide you with another piece of your family history puzzle. Likewise, one piece of property is often passed down from generation to generation and, as such, one deed could provide you with all the information you need to complete a particular family group chart.

Other information to look for in land records include the name of the land-owner's wife, his other relatives, where he previously lived, when he bought the land, and when he sold it. This information can, at the very least, give you an idea of the migratory patterns of your ancestors.

A Word of Caution

I have one very important word of caution to give you regarding any search you undertake that involves the property of one of your ancestors. You are bound to come across some information that you probably don't want to know about, as it will rekindle memories of the most embarrassing portion of this country's history: slavery. You may very well find that one of your ancestors was a slave owner. While slavery is clearly a despicable thing, the only advice that I can give you is to try and not be too judgmental about this very sore subject; regrettably, at one time many white people owned slaves, so your ancestor was not alone in this practice. At least, thank goodness, this chapter of American history has come to a close.

9

FEDERAL GOVERNMENT
RESEARCH SOURCES

The National Archives

On the Pennsylvania Avenue side of the National Archives building in Washington, D.C., there is an inscription that reads, "The heritage of the past is the seed that brings forth the harvest of the future." This should give you a clue as to just how valuable the records stored here are for anyone who is searching for their family roots.

There is an immense amount of information available to any genealogist in the National Archives as well as other institutions located in our nation's capitol, such as the Smithsonian, the Library of Congress, and the Immigration and Naturalization Service. From mortality census schedules to ships' passenger lists, from military records to census information, you are guaranteed to find some kind of record of any ancestor who ever lived in the United States. Perhaps this is why Washington, D.C. is often called "the capitol of genealogy."

If you are at least able to visit the National Archives in person—something every citizen should do once in his life if only to view such grand historical documents as the Declaration of Independence, the Bill of Rights, and the Constitution, among others—you will receive a free consultation with a member of the staff, who will be able to give you much needed advice in regards to researching your family roots while inside this palace of information.

If you can't make it to the National Archives in person, you can do one of two things. First, you can try requesting the information by mail. To do this, send a friendly, precise letter with your request to:

National Archives and Records Administration
Washington, D.C. 20408

Again, include a self-addressed, stamped envelope and offer to pay for any costs incurred in the search.

The other alternative you have if you are unable to travel to Washington, D.C. is to go to one of the National Archives regional branches, where you will find a great deal of the same information that is on file in the main branch. Here are the addresses:

For Alabama, Georgia, Florida, Kentucky, Mississippi, North Carolina, South Carolina, and Tennessee:
National Archives—Southeast Region
1557 St. Joseph Avenue
East Point, Georgia 30344

For Connecticut, Maine, Massachusetts, New Hampshire, Rhode Island, and Vermont:
National Archives—New England Region
380 Trapelo Road
Waltham, Massachusetts 02154

For Illinois, Indiana, Michigan, Minnesota, Ohio, and Wisconsin:
National Archives—Great Lakes Region
7358 South Pulaski Road
Chicago, Illinois 60629

For Colorado, Montana, North Dakota, South Dakota, Utah, and Wyoming:
National Archives—Rocky Mountain Region
Building 48, Denver Federal Center
P.O. Box 25307
Denver, Colorado 80225

For Arkansas, Louisiana, New Mexico, Oklahoma, and Texas:

National Archives—Southwest Region
501 West Felix Street
P.O. Box 6216
Fort Worth, TX 76115

For Iowa, Kansas, Missouri, and Nebraska:

National Archives—Central Plains Region
2312 East Bannister Road
Kansas City, Missouri 64131

For Arizona, Southern California, and Clark County, Nevada:

National Archives—Pacific Southwest Region
24000 Avila Road, 1st Floor
P.O. Box 6719
Laguna Niguel, California 92677

For New Jersey, New York, Puerto Rico, and Virgin Islands:

National Archives—Northeast Region
Building 22, Military Ocean Terminal
Bayonne, New Jersey 07002

For Delaware, Pennsylvania, District of Columbia, Maryland, Virginia, and West Virginia:

National Archives—Mid-Atlantic Region
9th and Market Streets, Room 1350
Philadelphia, Pennsylvania 19107

For Northern California, Hawaii, Nevada (with the exception of Clark County), and all territories in the Pacific:

National Archives—Pacific Sierra Region
1000 Commodore Drive
San Bruno, California 94066

For Idaho, Oregon, and Washington:
National Archives—Pacific Northwest Region
6125 Sand Point Way NE
Seattle, Washington 98115

For Alaska:
National Archives—Alaska Region
654 West Third Avenue, Room 012
Anchorage, AK 99501

Census Records

Census records are some of the most important government documents available to the genealogist. Through them you can trace the migratory patterns of your ancestors, the number of people in their households, and even discover other relatives through alternate spellings of names. No genealogy can ever be considered complete until the censuses of this country have been studied. Although they often contain mistakes (as will be discussed shortly), they are an excellent way of double-checking information gleaned from other sources.

The first censuses in America were instituted by the British government during the colonial period. Anxious to keep a close watch on profitable trade and taxes, the British monarchy insisted that fairly accurate records be kept of the colonists. As a result, the colonies took almost forty censuses of their populations between 1600 and 1789. Copies of all of these censuses are available for you to look at.

In 1790, the federal government administered the first official U.S. census. The reason for this was so that they could gauge the military power of the country in the event of war. Since then, they have administered a new census every ten years, compiling schedules of residents on a countywide basis within each state. Copies of these records until the year 1910 are also available for public perusal.

United States' censuses taken from 1920 to the present are not available to the public because of the Privacy Act of 1974 which stipulated that no federal records less than 75 years old be released to the public. However, if you write to the Bureau of the Census, Pittsburg, Kansas 66762, and request a census search, they will send you a form to fill out. By sending back the completed form and a small fee, you will receive a copy of the information contained on your ancestor's census records.

Here are a few helpful hints to keep in mind while searching through census files:

1) Be aware that censuses are not always accurate. There are several reasons for this. First, census takers were notoriously bad spellers. Even common names like Smith and Jones already had several different variants, but the census takers created even more through poor spelling. They usually spelled out names phonetically, and this became extremely problematic in regions where heavy accents were prevalent.

Moreover, as early census takers were paid by the number of interviews they conducted, they would sometimes invent families in order to earn extra money. If this seems reprehensible to you, then you should at least be aware that they were paid so poorly that many regions of the country were unable to hire enough census takers to complete the 1790 census until 1792! But the primary reason for inaccuracies is due to a general mistrust of census takers on the part of the public; people simply did not want to share their private lives with the government.

2) Begin with the 1910 census and work backwards, tracing your family line as far back as possible. Be sure to record all of the information available about your ancestors—whether or not it seems important at the time—onto your family group charts.

3) Always check out other families living in the same town or county and sharing the same last name as your ancestors—you might stumble upon some relatives you had never known about. Also, just because the children in the household share the same last name with the head of the household, don't assume that they are his children. They could be nephews, servants, cousins, etc. This is especially prevalent in the earlier censuses.

Now for the censuses themselves. Listed below are the contents of all of the censuses available to the public.

1790: This census lists the names of the heads of households, the number of free white males under and over 16 years old, the number of free white females, the number of free black people, and the number of slaves. Be wary of the figures quoted for the average number of family members living in the same household, as they often include such people as workers, friends, or boarders who were not actually members of the family. Also, when the British attacked Washington, D.C. during the War of 1812, the schedules for Delaware, Georgia, Kentucky, New Jersey, Tennessee, Virginia, and parts of Maryland and North Carolina were burned, although many of these lost records have been restored with the help of state tax lists.

1800: Contains the names of the heads of households, the number of free white males and females under the age of 10, and between the ages of 10 and

16, 16 and 26, 26 and 44, and over 44 years old. The census also lists the number of free black people and the number of slaves. The schedules for Georgia, Indiana Territory, Kentucky, Mississippi Territory, New Jersey, Northwest Territory Ohio River, Tennessee, and Virginia are entirely missing. The schedules for Maine, Maryland, Massachusetts, New Hampshire, Pennsylvania, and South Carolina are partially missing.

1810: This census lists the same information as the previous census. The schedules for District of Columbia, Georgia, Indiana Territory, Louisiana, Michigan, Mississippi, New Jersey, and Ohio are entirely missing. Those for Illinois Territory, Maine, New York, North Carolina, Pennsylvania, Tennessee, and Virginia are partially missing.

1820: This census lists the names of the heads of households, the number of free white males and females under 10 years old, between the ages of 10 and 16, 16 and 18, 18 and 26, 26 and 45, and over 45 years old. Also included are the number of naturalized aliens; the number of people working in the agricultural, commercial, and manufacturing industries; the number of free black people; the number of slaves; and the number of people (with the exception of Native Americans) who were not taxed. The schedules for Alabama, Arkansas Territory, Missouri, and New Jersey are entirely missing. Those for Georgia, Indiana, Maine, New Hampshire, North Carolina, Ohio, Pennsylvania, and Tennessee are partially missing.

1830: Contains the names of the heads of households, the number of free white people under 5 years old, 10 years old, 15 years old, 20 years old, 30 years

106

old, 40 years old, and so on up to the age of 100. The census also lists the number of people working in a variety of different professions; the city, county, town, parish, district, etc., where the census was taken; the names and ages of military veterans who received pensions; the number of deaf, dumb, and insane white and black people; the number of unnaturalized aliens; and a variety of information about schools. It goes on to list the number of free black people, as well as the number of slaves.

1840: This census lists the same information as the previous census, with the exception of number of unnaturalized citizens and information about schools.

1850, 1860: At this point, the censuses began to include a great deal more information. For every free person living in the household, there is a record of his name, address, age, sex, color, occupation (for those over 15 years old), value of real estate owned, place of birth (including the name of the state, territory, or county), marriage status, schooling, and the value of personal property. For each slave, there was a record of the owner of the slave, and the slave's age, sex, and color, as well as whether the slave was a fugitive or not. Also contained were the total amount of slaves set free by every owner.

1870: This census contains the same information as the previous two, as well as a listing of black people, Chinese people, and Native Americans by name. Also included are the exact month of all citizens either born or married within the year.

1880: Indexed alphabetically by name, this census records the name, age, sex, marital status, and color of every person in the household, as well as their relationship to the head of the household. Additionally, the place of birth of the father and mother of the people recorded in the census is also given.

1890: This census was almost entirely burned in a fire.

1900, 1910: The most complete censuses yet to be released, these two offer the genealogist all of the information included in the previous censuses, as well as the exact month and year of birth of every person living in the country.

As well as the federal censuses, most states have instituted their own censuses. Whenever possible, the census of the state in which your ancestor lived should be inspected, if only to try to verify the information from the federal census. The single best directory of such state records is John "D" Stemmons' *United States Census Compendium*. This book lists all of the various directories, tax lists, and other records that can serve as a census for each state, as well as directing you to the various archives, libraries, and offices which house them.

A census can be a fairly difficult document for the inexperienced genealogist to sift through and interpret—many censuses are not even compiled in alphabetical order, requiring you to look through every entry for each county in which you are interested. But the Bureau of the Census has published a wonderful book which can help you in your efforts. Entitled *A Century of Population Growth from the First Census of*

the United States to the Twelfth, 1790-1900, this publication has two very important sections. First, "Table 111,"
a chart inside the book, lists every variant for every
name found in the first twelve censuses. This can take
away a lot of guessing work, which is particularly
helpful when you consider that some names have over
twenty variants! And secondly, the book contains several maps indicating changes in boundaries as the
nation aged—you will remember how important this
is from your search of various cemeteries.

Here is an example of how a census can be useful
to you in your search. Suppose you are tracing an ancestor named Joseph Becker, a man who lived in Pennsylvania in the early 1800s with his wife, Sarah. Starting around 1830, his name has disappeared from all
local, state, and church records, but as you cannot find
a death certificate, you cannot simply assume that he
died. You go back to the federal census of 1820 and
you discover (fortunately) that the records for the
county in which he lived have not been lost. Joseph
Becker is listed as the head of a household, and one
woman between the age of 26 and 45 is documented
as living in the household. This woman is presum-
ably Sarah. You then go to the census of 1830, but you
can no longer find an entry for a Joseph Becker. This
census does, however, now list a Sarah Becker as the
head of a household, and it also reports that there is
one boy under the age of five in the household. From
this information, you can deduce two things. One,
Joseph Becker did indeed die, leaving Sarah Becker
as the head of the household. Two, he must have died
after 1825, as he had a son less than five years old in
1830. From this example, you can see that a census is
a very useful document, but that it requires you to
piece together information.

Mortality Census Schedules

I should mention the Mortality Census Schedules, which were first compiled in 1850. These schedules list the name, age, sex, marital status, place of birth, occupation, place of death, and cause of death of all individuals who passed away in the 12 month period prior to when the census was taken. These records can be found in state libraries and through certain historical societies, such as the Daughters of the American Revolution (1776 D Street, N.W., Washington, D.C.).

Military Records

Whenever you are searching through the volumes and volumes of old records necessary to complete a genealogy, it is very easy to lose sight of how exciting the process should be to you. One type of document that will definitely fill you with passion, however, is the military record. The United States has been involved in many conflicts in its short life, so the chances are extremely high that one or more of your male ancestors served in combat. Military documents allow you to relive the victories and losses of wars that have literally shaped the course of history. Just think, your ancestor could have played a decisive role in creating the world as we know it! These records will certainly add some color and spice to your genealogy.

The number of military records available at the National Archives alone is mind blowing. A partial summary (not including the documents you can find at state and local archives) follows:

1) Histories of officers
2) Service records for enlisted men in the Marines
3) Service records for the Army
4) Officer records for the Navy
5) Civil War records

6) Service records for enlisted men in the Navy
7) Muster rolls for the Army
8) Records of appointees to Annapolis
9) Officer records for the Army
10) Pay records
11) Mexican War records
12) Philippine Insurrection records
13) Coast Guard records (before 1915 this branch of the Armed Services was known as the Bureau of Light-houses)
14) Enlistment papers for the Army
15) Officer records for the Marines
16) Records for prisoners of war
17) Draft records for the Civil War
18) Spanish-American War records
19) Records of soldiers' burials
20) Records for the U.S. Military Academy

If all of this seems like a ridiculous amount of paperwork, then you have to remember that the United States has been involved in about a dozen wars! But don't worry, because it's not as difficult to sort out these records as it first appears. All of these different documents basically fall within three main categories of military records: the actual record of service itself, military pension applications, and land grant applications. All of these are excellent sources to utilize when trying to find genealogical information on your male ancestors. I will now go into more detail about each category.

Service Records

In order to obtain a service record, you must first figure out which war your ancestor served in. How do you go about doing this? Regrettably, there is no one answer to this question. You essentially have to rely on all of the other information you have already obtained. In some instances, this can be quite simple. For example, suppose that while you are interviewing some of your living relatives, one of them mentions that your grandfather served in World War I. You now know that you have to track down a WWI service record.

On the other hand, it can also be quite difficult. Suppose you've traced your family back to the 1840s, and you've discovered a birth certificate for an ancestor that you had never even heard of before, named John Becker. Obviously one of your living relatives isn't going to be able to help you out on this one. You will need to scour through all of the local, state, and church records that you have already found, looking for any references to John Becker's service in the Armed Forces. Personal records, such as diaries and entries in family Bibles, are especially helpful in finding such references. But suppose you find no indication that he ever joined the military. Does this automatically mean that you should not attempt to find a service record?

Absolutely not! In the above example you may have noticed that John Becker was born in the 1840s, meaning that he was in his twenties in the 1860s. If you are familiar with your American history, then you will remember that the Civil War lasted from 1861 to 1865. Therefore, the chances are very high that he fought in that war. So, even if you're just going on a hunch, it's still a good idea to search for service records. It's also probably a good idea for you to brush up on your American history, so that you are aware of the dates of all the wars and police actions in which America has been involved. The chart on the following page may be of some help to you.

112

Major American Military Conflicts

1775-1779	The Revolutionary War
1812-1815	The War of 1812
1846	The Mexican War
1861-1865	The Civil War
1898	The Spanish-American War
1914-1918	World War I
1939-1945	World War II
1950-1953	The Korean Conflict
1964-1972	The War in Vietnam
1990-1991	The Gulf War

The most important place to look for service records is in the National Archives in Washington, D.C. You should be aware that, as with census records, military documents are considered private for 75 years, so you can only request information specifically about your ancestor. As the process of obtaining these records can be a little confusing to the uninitiated, I suggest that you write to the National Archives and request their brochure entitled *Military Service Records in the National Archives of the United States.*

To obtain a copy of a service record, simply write to the National Archives and ask for a copy of NATF Form 80. Once you complete and mail back the form, a member of the National Archives' staff will conduct a search for your ancestor's records and mail you back copies of whatever he or she finds. There is usually a small photocopying fee for which you will be billed.

To obtain a copy of a service record for a veteran of the Civil War, you should also ask for a copy of NATF Form 80. But since the National Archives primarily houses the records of Union soldiers, if your ancestor served in the Confederacy, then the staff member may not be able to find any of his service records. If this happens, you should contact the state archives of the states which comprised the Confederacy and ask them to search their records. There is also an archive in the Confederate Memorial Building in Virginia.

To obtain a copy of a service record for a veteran of World War I, you should write to the National Archives Regional Archives, 1557 St. Joseph Avenue, East Point, GA 30344, and request more information.

To obtain a copy of a service record that is less than 75 years old, you need to write to the Department of Defense, Military Personnel Records, 9700 Page Blvd., St. Louis, MO 63132, and request a Standard Form 180. Please note that you must be related to the veteran whose information you are searching.

As you can see, it is actually quite simple to get a service record. All you have to know is which address to write to and which form to use. The more information that you can provide about your ancestor the better, but staff members can usually make do with the bare minimum. The amount of information that they can send back to you varies depending upon in which war your ancestor served (some older records are incomplete or lost), but it will surely be of help to you in constructing your genealogy.

Veterans Pensions

Probably the most important military records are pension applications. There are literally millions of such records, and the National Archives has divided them into seven categories: Revolutionary War invalid,

114

Revolutionary War service, Old Wars, War of 1812, Mexican War, Civil War and later, and Indian Wars.

Many pension applications contain a variety of information, including letters or affidavits from relatives, friends, and fellow soldiers, birth and marriage certificates . . . anything that would have added credibility to the veteran's pension claim. If the claim was filed by the veteran himself, then it most likely includes some of his vital statistics and a summary of his duties in the Armed Forces. If it was filed by his widow, then it also includes her vital statistics and the names of their dependents. If it was filed by a dependent, then it includes many of the dependent's vital statistics as well.

When trying to find your ancestor's pension application, you must be able to provide the National Archives' staff with the exact state and preferably town or county that your ancestor came from. There are too many duplicate names on file for any positive identification to be made without this information.

To get a copy of your ancestor's pension application file, or to find out if one of your ancestors has ever made such a claim, write the National Archives and request NATF Form 80, just as you would do for a military service record. When you receive a copy of the file, check to see if they have sent you the complete file or just one portion of it. If you feel there is more valuable information that was not sent to you, write back to the National Archives and ask them how much it will cost to obtain a copy of the complete file. They will let you know, and you can then decide if it is worth the fee—which can be fairly steep for such a request—for you to have this information.

Bounty Land Grants

Land grant applications comprise the final category of important military documents. Land grants were one of the many ways the government rewarded its veterans. Patriots (or their heirs) who fought in wars between the years 1775 and 1855 were entitled to land which was a part of the public domain. Besides providing an inducement for men to serve their country, land grants also brought about the migration of thousands of people to the wild, wild west.

Congress decreed on September 16, 1776, that each colonel was entitled to 500 acres of land; each lieutenant colonel, 450 acres; each captain, 300 acres; each lieutenant, 200 acres; each ensign, 150 acres; and each soldier, 100 acres of land.

Among the information contained in the land grant application files are the veteran's name, rank, unit, term of service, age, residence, and sometimes even a physical description of said applicant. If filed by an heir, the file should include the name of the veteran, the name of the heir, their relationship, and the place and date of the veteran's death.

Land grant applications are divided into two categories: Revolutionary War and post-Revolutionary War. To obtain a copy of your ancestor's file, write to the National Archives and request that all-important NATF Form 80.

Passenger Lists and Naturalization Records

With passenger lists, it is possible to find out when your ancestors arrived in the United States as well as what country they left from to get here. In general, the only surviving lists are from the years 1820 through 1945, and from the ports located on the Atlantic Coast or the Gulf of Mexico. The lists from the San Francisco port were destroyed by a series of fires over the years, while records from the late 18th and early 19th centuries are just plain scarce.

Passenger lists were first compiled extensively in the early 1800s, when stricter regulation of immigration was put into effect. Over the years, the amount of information with which passengers had to supply customs officials increased dramatically, which means that some of the lists that are available contain a wealth of genealogical information.

Passenger lists, which were filled out by a ship's captain, usually contain the name of the captain and the ship, the port of embarkation, the name of the port, the date of the ship's arrival, and the name, age, sex, and occupation of each passenger.

Because of the many problems which confront the genealogist who is searching through passenger lists— illegible writing, gaps in the records, incomplete information and indexing—it is imperative that you know the name of the ship your ancestor came on, the name of the port of entry, and the arrival date (approximate as best you can). With this data, the staff of the National Archives might be able to find the information you are looking for.

But how can you even find out all of these facts that you need to give to the National Archives? There are several excellent books available that list the names of millions of passengers who arrived in this country by ship and the dates of their arrival. Some are indexed in such a way that you can clearly determine who was related to whom, and who traveled together with whom. I highly recommend *Passenger Lists Bibliography* (P. William Filby, editor) and *Adler's Directory: A Compilation of Passenger Steamships Sailing from European Ports and Arriving in the Eastern Ports of the United States from 1899-1929.*

The following are some of the other most noteable and readily available passenger lists:

Browning, Charles. *Welsh Settlement of Pennsylvania.*

Farmer, John. *A Genealogical Register of the First Settlers of New England.*

Hotten, John. *The Original List of Persons of Quality Who Went from Great Britain to the American Plantations, 1600-1700.*

Joseph, Samuel. *Jewish Immigration to the United States from 1881 to 1910.*

Kaminkow, Jack. *A list of Emigrants from England to America, 1719-1759.*

Strassburger, Ralph. *Pennsylvania German Pioneers: Port of Philadelphia from 1727 to 1808.*

Yoder, Donald. *Emigrants from Wyer Hemberg; the Adolf Gerber Lists.*

Naturalization records might be able to help you in your search for passenger lists, and vice-versa. In other words, if you know the name of the court where your ancestor was naturalized (this can be learned from the list of voters in the county where he lived), you can gain access to his naturalization records, which will tell you the date and the port of his arrival. Likewise, if you have enough information to get a hold of the passenger list of the ship on which your ancestor arrived, you should have no problem obtaining his naturalization records.

To receive a copy of your ancestor's naturalization records, write to the Immigration and Naturalization Service, 119 D Street, N.W., Washington, D.C. 20536 and request form N-585. After filling out and returning this form, you will be sent a file with the information you need.

A very valuable book which may help you in lo-

118

cating naturalization documents that are unavailable through the Immigration and Naturalization Service (some older records are in the National Archives, some are in local archives, and some are even still in local courthouses) is John J. Newman's *American Naturalization Process and Procedures, 1790-1985.*

Miscellaneous Records

Three other very important federal records exist that can help you on your genealogical search: social security records, passport applications, and registration records for Americans abroad.

The Social Security Administration mandates that all applicants for benefits provide their date and place of birth. As the administration came into existence in the 1930s, people born in the mid-1800s onward are documented in their files. If one of your ancestors who immigrated to this country has Social Security records, then this information could allow you to trace your roots back to your ancestral homeland.

In order to gain access to the Social Security Administration's files, you have to provide either your ancestor's Social Security number or his death certificate. Send your inquiries to: The Social Security Administration, 6401 Security Blvd., Baltimore, MD 21235.

Modern passports are documents which guarantee a citizen the right to visit foreign countries. But early passports were also for domestic use, allowing an individual to travel between states and territories. These documents include the individual's name, date of birth, where he lives, and a photograph (after the advent of photography). The State Department, which is responsible for U.S. passports, sends all processed passport applications to the National Archives.

119

Finally, early in the 20th century, U.S. consulates abroad began registering the names, dates of birth, and places of birth of all U.S. citizens living in foreign countries. These registration records are available through the National Archives. They could be crucial in your genealogical search if one of your ancestors spent a few years outside of the U.S.

Hiring a Professional Genealogist— The Right Decision for You?

By now you have probably realized that tracing your genealogy can become quite complex if you are striving to put together a complete, comprehensive family history. You may have to do some traveling. You may have to translate some foreign text. You may have to dig through volumes and volumes of information. As a result, you might come to a point where you decide that it is time to hire a professional genealogist. You might arrive at this decision because you feel that you do not possess some of the skills necessary to adequately complete your search, but I hope that you won't do so simply because you feel you don't have the time to spare. After all, if you can't make time to personally find out about your heritage, what can you find time for? Ideally, *you* should be the one to trace your heritage, as it will allow you to make new discoveries about your past and find out more about yourself in the process. Why hire a professional when it will mean losing the bond that you wish to create with your ancestors? Nonetheless, if you feel that you absolutely require the services of a professional genealogist, then you should expect the following:

1) An initial consultation with the professional, in which you provide him with any information you have already acquired. He should examine this infor-

mation with you, so that you can discuss with him exactly what additional information you want him to provide.

2) The professional genealogist should search through all available records for you, essentially performing the various searches that I have already presented in this book. As this search may require certain special skills, you have the right to ask him about his qualifications. What foreign languages can he speak? Is he especially familiar with the archives in a particular area?

3) The professional genealogist should fill out your ancestral and family group charts, thus putting together a genealogy for you. All new sources of information should be cited (or photocopied, if possible), and he should provide a detailed invoice of all expenses incurred during the search.

4) At the initial consultation, the professional genealogist should clearly outline his fees (including any hidden costs), how long he is willing to work on your genealogy, and when he can start.

Professional genealogists can be hired by contacting the following agencies:

The Genealogical Society of the Church
of Jesus Christ of Latter Day Saints
Suite 1006
54 East South Temple Street
Salt Lake City, UT 84111

The Board of Certification of Genealogists
1307 New Hampshire Avenue, N.W.
Washington, D.C. 20036

WARNING! You will also probably find certain professionals advertised in some of the genealogical journals that you read; these journals extensively research the people who advertise in their pages, so there is little chance of being cheated by one of these professionals. But be wary of any "professional" whom you see advertising in any other kind of periodical, as a high percentage of them are frauds. They usually compile a single genealogy for everyone with the same last name, never bothering to check if this is truly your line of descent.

If you ever feel cheated by a professional that you hire, there is an agency that can help you with your dispute. Simply contact the Association of Professional Genealogists, Box 11601, Salt Lake City, UT 84101. They will advise you on how best to proceed.

10

SEARCHING FOR YOUR ANCESTORS IN FOREIGN COUNTRIES

Begin at Home

Any search for your ancestral homeland should begin right here in the United States. Before spending the money, time, and energy that goes into traveling overseas, you should gather all the information you possibly can about the ancestors and the countries you will be researching.

To begin with, you will at least need to know the name of your ancestor, the country and city where he came from, and the approximate date of his immigration. The next step would be to contact the LDS library in Salt Lake City, or one of their regional branches in your area, to see what kind of information they have about your ancestor in their files. You'll be pleasantly surprised to know that, along with their vast collection of American genealogical records, the LDS library has a sizable amount of information on countries who have supplied the United States with immigrants.

The staff at the LDS library will also provide you with the addresses of foreign agencies who may be able to supply you with the records of birth, death, marriage, etc., for which you will ultimately be searching. If, for some reason, the LDS library does not have the addresses for the particular country in which you are interested, or if the agencies overseas prove to be of no help, try writing to the American embassy in the country or city you are interested in researching and ask them if they can be of assistance.

In general, you should conduct all of your foreign correspondence just as you would do in the United States; after all, most countries have the same type of record keeping system as we do, with census data, military information, tax records, etc., all readily available. Always remember to include enough interna-

124

tional reply coupons to cover the cost of having your overseas connection answer any of your inquiries.

While searching for your family roots in foreign countries is a highly challenging and sometimes frustrating experience, the rewards of such a search defy description. To be able to walk on the same ground that your ancestor stepped on hundreds of years ago, to correspond with a distant relative in a far away country, to discover that your ancestor was a famous artist or writer whose works you've always admired but to whom you never dreamed you were related . . . these experiences are like no other, as they link you to other worlds and other lifetimes that you perhaps never even knew existed but are actually as much a part of you as the small town or neighborhood in which you grew up.

List of Sources, Country by Country

The following is a list of resources that are available to you while tracing your roots in a foreign country. Naturally, you only need to read the sections pertaining to the countries from which your ancestors came, unless you are asked to refer to another section for additional information. I must stress at this point that you should definitely familiarize yourself with the histories of the countries from which your ancestors came before you begin searching for your roots; a little extra research now will help you out more than you can ever imagine once your search has begun!

Australia

You may want to begin your search in Australia by writing to the Genealogical Society of Victoria, Room 1, 1st Floor, 98 Elizabeth St., Melbourne, Victoria 3000 and requesting their helpful book, *Ancestors for*

Australians. When searching for vital records, you will need to know in which state or territory your ancestor was born and/or lived. Here are the addresses for the archives for the six different states and the two territories:

1) For Australian Capital Territory: The Registrar, Birth, Death and Marriage Registry, P.O. Box 788, Camberra, ACT, 2601.

2) For New South Wales: The Registrar-General, Births, Deaths and Marriages Branch, Prince Albert Road, Sydney, NSW, 2000.

3) For Northern Territory: The Registrar-General, Births, Deaths and Marriages Branch, P.O. Box 3094, Darwin, NT, 5794.

4) For Queensland: The Registrar-General, Treasury Buildings, Brisbane, B7, Queensland, 4000.

5) For South Australia: The Principal Registrar, Box 1351H, GPO Adelaide, SA, 5001.

6) For Tasmania: The Registrar-General, Box 875J, Hobart, Tasmania, 7001.

7) For Victoria: The Government Statist, 295 Queen Street, Melbourne, Victoria, 3000.

8) For Western Australia: The Registrar-General, Oakleigh Building, 22 St. George's Terrace, Perth, WA, 6000.

Austria

Like most other European countries, the recording of vital events in Austria began in local parishes. Ministers started documenting such events during the 16th century, and they continued to do so until 1938. There are so many Catholic parishes in the country that you will have to read the *Austrian Office Calendar* in order to pinpoint the one where your ancestor worshipped; you can find this book in better genealogical libraries, such as the LDS library in Utah. To find the records of a Protestant ancestor contact The High Church Council, Vienna I, Schellinggasse 12, Austria.

In order to find civil documents, your best approach is to contact the registrars of the town in which your ancestor lived. Not only do these registrars possess civil documents of vital events from 1938 onward, but they can also help you locate census records, obituaries, naturalization records, and various passport registers.

You might also want to do some research into the Hamburg passenger lists (see the section on Germany for more information) as many Austrians who emigrated departed from that port.

Belgium

Starting in about the 1600s, the Catholic clergy kept vital records for the citizens of Belgium. These records are now available in town halls and state archives. They are generally divided by parish or community, so if you are aware of the area where your ancestor lived, the task of finding his records shouldn't be too difficult. In 1795, civil registration began, and most civil records can now be found at town and commune halls.

For assistance in tracing your genealogy, or for certain other records (such as various probate documents), contact Les Archives Generales du Royaume, rue de Ruysbroeck 2-6 1000, Brussels, Belgium.

Canada

Canada does not keep its civil registration records in one central office. Instead, vital statistics are filed with provincial and territorial offices. However, the Public Archives of Canada at 395 Wellington St., Ottawa, Ontario K1A 0N3, can help you in your search. They also publish some excellent publications, including "Genealogical Sources at the Public Archives of Canada," and "Tracing Your Ancestors in Canada." To inquire about such publications, write to the Publications Division, Public Archives of Canada, Postal Station B, 59 Sparks and Elgin, 6th Floor, Ottawa, Ontario K1A 0N3.

If you know the province or territory from which your ancestor hails, you may contact one of the following registrars:

1) For Alberta: Director of Vital Statistics, Department of Health and Social Development, Edmonton, T5N 0M6.

2) For British Columbia: Division of Vital Statistics, Department of Health Services and Hospital Insurance, Victoria, V8V 1X4.

3) For Manitoba: The Recorder, Division of Vital Statistics, Department of Health and Social Development, Winnipeg, R3C 0P8.

4) For New Brunswick: The Registrar General, Department of Health, Fredericton, E3B 5H1.

5) For Newfoundland: Registrar of Vital Statistics, Department of Health, St. John's, A1C 5E2.

6) For North West Territories: Registrar General of Vital Statistics, Yellowknife, N.W. T. X1A 2L9.

7) For Nova Scotia: The Registrar General, Department of Public Health, Halifax, B3H 1Z9.

8) For Ontario: Deputy Registrar General, Macdonald Block, Queen's Park, Toronto, M7A 1C7.

9) For Prince Edward Island: Division of Vital Statistics, Department of Health, Charlottetown, C1A 7M4.

10) For Quebec: Registrar General, Population Register, Department of Social Affairs, Quebec City.

11) For Saskatchewan: Director of Vital Statistics, Department of Public Health, Regina, S4S 0A2.

If you are interested in researching church records in Canada, you should write to the Untied Church of Canada, Committee on Archives, Victoria University, Queen's Park Crescent East, Toronto, Ontario M5S 1K7. For Anglican Church records, write to the Anglican Church of Canada, 600 Jarvis Street, Toronto, Ontario, M4Y 2J6.

China, The Peoples Republic of

Tracing your genealogy in China is much different than finding your roots in Europe. Due to the extreme importance of ancestor worship in China (as well as in other Asian countries), it is quite possible to find an already completed genealogy. The availability of written public records, however, is a problematic issue for two reasons. First, during the 1950s the government of China burned many documents that it considered "dangerous." And second, although the government encourages people to return to China and trace their roots, they are very strict about releasing the remaining documents to the public.

There are several sources of information which will probably be very useful to you. As noted above, families often diligently record their lineage in homage to their ancestors, so if you can contact any living relatives in China, then they will most certainly give you access to their *private* genealogical records. You should also visit cemeteries and ancestral worshipping halls, the walls of which are often adorned with the names of forebears.

There is one important type of civil document of which you may be able to obtain a copy. A *fang-chih* is a local history in which the names and accomplishments of important people are recorded. At the very least this will be fascinating reading, providing you with a solid knowledge of the area where your ancestor lived, but you might even discover that your ancestor is mentioned in the document.

You should not forget to write to the Chief Librarian of the National Central Library in Taipei, Taiwan. The Taiwanese government encourages families to publish their genealogies, and you may find valuable information there.

Before pursuing any other leads, you should definitely read a pamphlet called *The Extent and Preservation of Genealogical Records in China*, by Professor Hsiang-lin Lo. It is readily available at the LDS library, and it is filled with good suggestions on how you can get started.

Czechoslovakia

Although Czechoslovakia has been peacefully divided into two countries, it is not yet certain how the archival material will be divided. As a result, I have decided to present you with the information as if it were still one country.

Catholic and Protestant clergymen began recording vital events in the 17th century, and your ancestor's records are still available in the local parish where he worshipped. Civil authorities began recording vital events in 1950, and these records are available in the central archives. Write to Statni Ustredni Archiv, Karmelitska 2 Prague I. The Czech and Slovak embassies can also help you find any information you need, but they do charge a small fee.

If you have any questions regarding Czech documents, write to Ceskoslovensky ustav zahranicni, Karmelitska 25, Prague 1. If you have any questions regarding Slovakian documents, write to Matica Slovenska Nositerka Radu Republicky, Oddelenie pre zahranicnych Slovakov, Pugacevova 2, Bratislava 1.

Denmark

Continuing in the trend of other Scandinavian countries, when tracing your roots in Denmark, you must be aware of the importance of church records from local parishes, and of the existence of patronymics (please refer to the section on Sweden for more information).

Vital events were traditionally recorded by parish ministers, and some records date back to the 17th century. In 1814 the records became standardized. Vital records and probate documents can be found in any of the following regional archives:

1) For Fyn: Landsarkivet, 36 Jerbanegade, DK 5000, Odense, Denmark.

2) For de sonderjyske Landsdele: Landsarkivet, 45 Haderslevvej, DK 6200, Abenra, Denmark.

3) For Sjaelland m.m.: Landsarkivet, 10 Jagtvej, DK 2200, Copenhagen N, Denmark.

4) For Norrejylland: Landsarkivet, 5L1. Sct. Hansgade, DK 8800, Viborg, Denmark.

The Danish National Archives (the Riksarkivet) is one of your key genealogical sources. There you can find all census information that is available to the public from 1787 onward. Censuses give the full name, age, relationship, occupation, residence, and marital status of everyone in the household. The Riksarkivet also stores all military records. You can reach the Riksarkivet by writing to The Danish National Archives, 9 Rigsdagsgarden, DK 1218, Copenhagen K, Denmark.

In order to find immigration records, simply write to The Danes Worldwide Archives, 2 Konvalvej, DK 9000, Alborg, Denmark. The immigration records housed there are quite extensive and can supply you with much genealogical information.

If you have any other questions, you should write to the Department of the Ministry of Foreign Affairs of Denmark, 2 Stormgade, DK-1470 Copenhagen K, Denmark, and request their free brochure, *Tracing Your Danish Ancestors and Relatives*.

England

Before contacting anyone else in your search for your roots in England, there are two offices that you should write to for information. First, the British Tourist Authority has produced an informative pamphlet, entitled *Tracing Your Ancestors in Britain*, that may help you in your quest. It is available free of charge by writing to The British Tourist Authority, 40 West 57th Street, New York, NY 10019. Second, you should contact the Society of Genealogists, which may be able to help you narrow down the sources available to you. They can be reached at The Society of Genealogists, 37 Harrington Gardens, Kensington, London, SW74JX, England.

Although vital record keeping began in England in the 1500s, civil registration did not start until 1837. If you wish to find any of the civil records for your ancestor, write to The Register General, St. Catherine's House, 10 Kingsway, London, WC2B6JP, England. For copies of any documents, it is best to give the staff as much information as possible. In the case of birth certificates, you should try to provide the entire name, the exact date and place of birth, and the full names of both parents. For death certificates, give the full name, exact date and place of death, marital status, and age. For marriage certificates, provide the date and place of marriage, and the full names of both bride and groom. If you are unable to provide this information, the staff will do their best to try and find the appropriate documents.

For vital records that date prior to 1837, you will have to search through church archives. Records were maintained by local parishes, so if you know the particular parish where your ancestor worshipped, it is best to address all queries there. If you do not know which parish to search, then you can write to the Society of Genealogists at the above address. This society has copies of almost every record contained in each local parish. But as they have so many records in their archives, it may take their staff some time to locate the information you need.

If your family did not belong to the Church of England, you can still track down documents from before 1837. Catholic records can be found at The Catholic Record Society, 5-24 Lennox Gardens, Westminster, London SWIX ODQ, England. For Jewish records, contact The Archives of the United Synagogue, Office of the Chief Rabbi, Adler House, Tavistock Square, London, WC1 9HN, England. Many Baptist records are located at Dr. William's Library, 14 Gordon Square, London, WC1H OAG, England. Huguenot records can be found at The Huguenot Society, 67 Victoria Road, London, WC1A ILH. For all other religions, check with the Society of Genealogists.

Probate records that are dated after 1958 are available from The Principal Probate Registry, Somerset House, Strand, London, W.C. 2. For records earlier than this, you will have to search through regional court houses.

Censuses from the years 1841, 1851, and 1861 can be found at the LDS library in Utah. Later censuses are not available to the public.

Finland

Unlike other Scandinavian countries, Finland never ascribed to the patronymic naming system (please see the section on Sweden for more information). Instead, the father's first name became the son's middle name, and his surname reflects his occupation or location. But Finland *is* like other Scandinavian countries in the importance it has traditionally placed on church records from local parishes.

In the 1600s, parish ministers began recording vital events. Civil records only came into effect at the end of World War I, and Finnish citizens are not required to use them. If they wish, they may still record vital events solely through the church.

For church records that were written after 1850, the individual parish where your ancestor worshipped must be sought out. For records written prior to 1850, or for civil records, you should contact The National Archives, Valtionarkisto/Riksarkivet PL274, SF-00171, Helsinki, 17, Finland.

France

France offers the genealogist a gold mine of information. Not only does this country have some of the oldest records in Europe, but after the French Revolution an accurate and systematic civil registration of vital events commenced. The National Archives of France (60 rue des Francs-Bourgeois, 75141 Paris CEDEX 03, France) is the storehouse for many important documents, and its staff can answer most of your questions.

Vital records were maintained by local clergymen until the end of the 18th century. These documents are now housed in regional (*departement*) archives, the addresses of which can be found through the National Archives. Therefore, if you are aware of the area where your ancestor lived, tracking down his records should not be too difficult. The civil records that were introduced at the end of the 18th century can be obtained by writing to the mayor of the town where your ancestor lived.

If your ancestor was Protestant, then you may wish to search for some records at La Bibliotheque de la Societe d'histoire du Protestantisme Francais, 54 rue des Saint-Pierres, 75 Paris 07, France.

Probate records that go back over 600 years are available at the National Archives. For some newer records, you will have to go to the local archives, so you might want to consult with the staff at the National Archives about tracking them down.

Army records and immigration documents are available at the National Archives. After 1836, censuses were taken on a town-by-town basis every five years, and these records are located at the *departement* archives of the town in which your ancestor lived.

Germany

Germany poses an interesting problem to the genealogist: now that the country is once again reunited, will its genealogical records ever be complete? The East German Ministry of Culture was notorious at insisting that East Germans had no interest in genealogical research, so it is possible that many records were destroyed. The future of genealogical tracing in Germany is, therefore, at once exciting and possibly tragic.

But the separation between East and West Germany was not the first time the country had been divided up. From the early-1400s to the late 1800s, there were rifts in Germany due to tensions between Catholics and Protestants, as well as to internal boundaries.

Before embarking on any serious genealogical study in Germany, it is *essential* to know whether your ancestor was Catholic or Protestant. Local parishes began to record vital events in the 1550s, and this continued until 1875. In 1876, church records were replaced with civil registration of vital events; the community was the basic unit of this civil registration and, as a result, each town houses an archives and a registrar's office (Standesamt). Each province also has an archive, in which you might find more genealogical records about your ancestor. As you can see, it is also very important for you to know the town in which your ancestor was born.

Emigration records can be a key to finding your roots in Germany. The most important port between the years 1850 and 1930 was Hamburg. The passenger records from this port indicate not only the passenger's name and residence, but also his destination, occupation, the names of people traveling with him, and the name of the ship on which he sailed.

Professional genealogists consider Germany to be one of the most difficult countries in which to trace your roots. As I mentioned in the previous chapter, I hope that you will not resort to hiring a professional simply to save you time, but in the case of Germany, you might need to do so in order to produce any results at all. At the very least, you should familiarize yourself with such books as *American Genealogical Resources in German Archives*.

For more information on finding your roots in Germany, I suggest you contact Verlag Degener & Company, a publisher of some of the most impressive genealogical books ever written. For a free catalog, write to Verlag Degener & Company, D 8530 Neustadt A.D. (Aisch), Germany. Specify whether you want to receive the catalog in German or English.

Greece

The key to finding your ancestor's records in Greece is knowing in which town he was born. Church records of vital events have been kept since the early 1800s, and civil records of vital events are available since 1925. The church records are still kept in the local parishes where they were documented. The civil records are kept in a town's local archive or registry. For help in tracking down the parish where your ancestor worshipped, write to The Greek Orthodox Archdiocese, 21 Aghias Filotheis Street, Athens, Greece. For information about civil documents, write to The Civil Registration Division, Ministry of the Interior, 57 Panepistimiou Street, Athens, Greece.

After an individual's death, his probate records are sent to the Secretary of the Court of the First Instance in Athens. This agency can help you find any probate records you need.

Hungary

Hungary, much like Germany and Austria, began recording vital events in local parishes. Ministers from both the Roman Catholic and Reformed churches were responsible for documenting the vital events of individuals between the years 1695 and 1895. To obtain copies of these church records, you must contact the parish where your ancestor worshipped.

Civil authorities took over the responsibility of recording vital events in 1895. Civil records are generally found in the registrars of the town in which an individual was born, but you can get copies of your ancestor's records from The Republic of Hungary Embassy, 3910 Shoemaker Street NW, Washington, D.C. 20008. The embassy can also help you find copies of Hungary's censuses, which list such facts as the number of people in a household, their names, ages, occupations, and religions.

As many Hungarians who emigrated left their country via the port in Hamburg, you should also take a look at the Hamburg passenger lists (see the section on Germany for more information).

Iceland

Since Iceland fell under Danish rule for almost 600 years, their system of records is very similar to that of Denmark. Vital events have been recorded by local parish ministers since 1746, and these documents can be found in the National Archives, Thjodskjalasfn Islands, Hver Fisgate 17, Reykjavik, Iceland. Probate records can also be found there.

Censuses have been taken every ten years since 1703, noting such facts as name, occupation, residence, age, and marital status. These censuses are available at the National Archives.

Incidentally, you should be aware that Iceland is the only Scandinavian country that continues to use the patronymic naming system (please see the section on Sweden for more information).

Ireland, Northern

The Northern Ireland Tourist Board publishes a very useful handbook entitled *Tracing Your Ancestry in Ulster*. The handbook is available free of charge by writing to The Northern Ireland Tourist Board, River House, 48 High Street, Belfast, BT 12DS, Northern Ireland.

For vital records, write to The General Register Office, Oxford House, 49-55 Chichester Street, Belfast, BT1 4HF, Northern Ireland. For vital records that date prior to 1922, you might also want to check in the General Register Office in Dublin, Republic of Ireland (please refer to the following section on the Republic of Ireland).

Church records are housed at local parishes. They date back to the beginning of the 18th century, but they contain many gaps. Presbyterian documents can be found at The Presbyterian Historical Society, Church House, Fisherwick Place, Belfast, Northern Ireland.

Surviving probate records are available at The Public Record Office for Northern Ireland, Law Courts Building, May Street, Belfast, Northern Ireland. The Public Record Office also has tax and voting records, and many parish registers for churches of various denominations.

Ireland, Republic of

Since the 1920s, Ireland has been divided into the Republic of Ireland, which is an independent country, and Northern Ireland, which falls under British rule. When searching for Irish records that pre-date the 1920s, you are best advised to check both Irelands, as documents could easily have wound up in the wrong place.

Irish history has been incredibly violent and, as a result, a great many genealogical records have been destroyed. Like Northern Ireland, until the 1920s the Republic of Ireland fell under British rule. Therefore, the records for members of the Church of Ireland (a Protestant church similar to the Church of England) are sometimes easier to find than those for Catholics, the other popular religion of the country.

Records of vital events since the 1860s can be found at The Registrar-General, The Custom House, Dublin, 1, Republic of Ireland. You should be aware that these records are in Latin.

Most of the censuses taken before 1901 were almost entirely lost. Copies of the portions that remain are available at the LDS library in Utah.

Church records for either Protestants or Catholics are most easily found in the local parishes. If you are unaware of the particular parish where your ancestor worshipped, you should contact The Public Record Office of Ireland (Oifig Iris Puibli), Four Courts, Dublin, 7, Republic of Ireland.

Probate records that date from the early-18th century onward are available at The Registry of Deeds, Henrietta Street, Dublin, 1, Republic of Ireland.

The Genealogical Office (2 Kildare Street, Dublin, 2, Republic of Ireland) might be able to track down some of your ancestor's records. Also, each county in the Republic of Ireland sponsors a Research Centre which can assist genealogists in finding the information they need. These Centres can be extremely helpful, particularly when it comes to making sense out of church records. They can be contacted through The Irish Tourist Board, 757 Third Ave., New York, NY 10017.

Italy

It is relatively easy to piece together a genealogy in Italy if you know the town where your ancestor was born. Italy has been fragmented many times during the course of its history and, as a result, records are stored locally, rather than centrally. Civil registration of vital events began around 1870, and these records can be tracked down through the registrar of the town in which your ancestor was born. The information on these civil records is wonderfully thorough, providing, for example, the names of several generations of ancestors. The local registrar should also be able to provide you with copies of *anagrafes*, or community censuses. For national censuses, contact The Istituto Centrale di Statistica, Via Cesare Balbo 16 00100, Rome, Italy.

Church records of vital events continued even after civil registration was implemented. These records are housed in local parishes, but they can be quite difficult to get at. Not only do you need to know Latin, but you will also have to muddle your way through piles and piles of unindexed documents.

Probate records from this century can usually be found through the registrar of the town in which your ancestor lived. For older records, contact The Archivio Notarile, Ispettatore Generale, Via Flaminia 160, Roma, Italy.

There are also nine state archives that might be able to help you with any questions you have. They are located in Bologna, Genoa, Turin, Palermo, Rome, Florence, Milan, Venice, and Naples.

Japan

As with China, Japanese religion and culture has encouraged the preservation of family genealogies in order to honor and worship ancestors. Therefore, tracing your roots is remarkably simple.

Japan has a strict Family Registration Law, in which all of the vital events of an individual's life are recorded in a uniform manner. Such a law is the genealogist's heaven.

In order to obtain copies of your ancestor's records, simply request your family register (*koseki*) from the village, city, or county office where your ancestor lived. There is a fee for these copies, so you should make arrangements for payment in advance.

The Genealogical Society of Japan (Nihon Keifu Gakkai), 3, 2-chome, Nakatsu Hondori, Oyodo-ku, Osaka, and the Japan Genealogical Association (Nihon Kakei Kyokai), 8-4, 3-chome, Ginza, Chuo-ku, Tokyo, are both very useful organizations to contact if you have any questions.

Mexico

Before you begin researching Mexican or Latin American ancestors, you should contact the LDS library in Salt Lake City, where many civil records and church registers from Mexico and Latin America have been copied onto microfilm. Once you have exhausted the material at the LDS library, you will probably want to write to Mexico's National Archives at Archivo General de la Nacion, Palacio Nacional, Mexico 1, D.F. They should be able to direct you to their own census records or to the Catholic parish archives in the various municipalities where birth, marriage, and death records have been kept throughout the centuries.

The Netherlands

Vital events have been documented by the clergy of the Netherlands since the late-1500s. The Catholic church had its main following in the south of the country, and the Dutch Reformed church was popular in the north. These records were extremely accurate, and they will be one of your most valuable genealogical tools.

You should be aware that patronymics (see the section on Sweden for an explanation) were in use until 1811, when the Emperor Napoleon introduced a true surname system. As a result, the entire population of the Netherlands simply chose new surnames. Fortunately, the names were generally similar in each area of the country, enabling you to deduce the area where your ancestor was born simply by knowing his name.

By 1795 in the south and 1811 in the north, civil registration had legally replaced the use of church records. All vital records, be they church or civil, can now be found through The Central Archive of the State, Algemeen Rijksarchief, Bleijenburg 7, The Hague. If the particular record you are tracing is not located there, then the staff will introduce you to the appropriate regional archive. All records are extensively indexed to make your search quicker and easier.

The Bevolking (population) register is essentially a census which can help trace the genealogy of every citizen of the Netherlands back to the year 1811.

In 1847, national emigration lists were compiled, indicating a passenger's name, marital status, residence, destination, and age. Three years later, when emigration boomed, entire towns began maintaining registers of their citizenry, so that their populations could be monitored.

Norway

Tracing your ancestors in Norway is much like finding your roots in Sweden. You should be aware of the importance of church records from local parishes, and of the existence of the patronymic naming system until the end of the 19th century (please see the previous section on Sweden for more information).

The first census in Norway was a head-tax list compiled in 1664. Censuses with varying degrees of accuracy have been kept ever since. They can be found in the National Archives, Riksarkivet, Bankplassen 3, Oslo 1, Norway.

As vital events were not recorded by the federal government of Norway until the mid-1940s, you will probably spend most of your time searching through church records. Parish ministers began recording vital events in the late-1600s, and these documents are moved to one of seven regional archives every eighty years. The archives also keep immigration records which indicate a passenger's name, address, departure date, and final destination. The following is a list of the archives, along with the areas they serve:

1) For Hedmark and Oppland: *Statsarkivet i Hamar*, Strandgata 71, N-2300 Hamar, Norway.

2) For Rogaland: *Statsarkivet i Stavanger*, Domkirkeplassen 1, N-4000 Stavanger, Norway.

3) For More og Romsdal, Sor-Trondelag, Nord-Trondelag, Nordland, Troms, and Finmark: *Statsarkivet i Trondheim*, Hogskoleveien 12, N-7000, Trondheim, Norway.

4) For Ostfold, Akershus, Oslo, Buskerud, Vestfold, and Telemark: *Statsarkivet i Oslo*, Prinsens gate 7-9, Oslo 1, Norway.

5) For Aust-Agder and Vest-Agder: *Statsarkivet i Kristiansand*, Vesterveien 4, N-4600 Kristiansand S, Norway.

6) For Hordaland, Sogn, and Fjordane: *Statsarkivet i Bergen*, Arstadveien 22, N-5000 Bergen, Norway.

7) For Troms and Finmark: *Statsarkivkontoret i Tromso*, Peterborggata 21-29, N-9000, Tromso, Norway.

The regional archives also keep probate records that date back to the mid-1600s. These records are quite specific in their estimates of land owned and division of land after death. Property deeds are available in both the regional archives and the National Archives. Military records can mostly be found in the National Archives.

You can order a wonderful pamphlet free of charge called *How to Trace Your Ancestors in Norway*. Simply write to The Royal Norwegian Ministry of Foreign Affairs, Office of Cultural Relations, Oslo, Norway. You might also find it helpful to write to the Norwegian-American Historical Association, St. Olaf College, Northfield, MN 55057.

Poland

Despite the violent political upheavals that have occurred in Poland throughout the last few centuries, tracing your Polish genealogy is surprisingly straightforward due to the help you can receive from certain key offices.

To obtain copies of your ancestor's vital records contact the United States Embassy in Warsaw. For a small fee, the staff will help you track down documents dating back to 1870, when civil registration of vital events officially began. Prior to this time, vital events were documented by local ministers, and you will have to contact the parish where your ancestor worshipped if you want to obtain these older records. For this reason, it is extremely useful if you know your ancestor's religion.

To find the addresses of these parishes, as well as to examine a host of relevant genealogical material on your Polish ancestors, you should contact the two main archives in Warsaw. For records that date prior to 1945, write to The Archiwum Glowne Akt Dawnych, Warsaw, Dluga 7, Poland. For records after 1945, contact The Archiwum Akt Nowych, Warsaw, Dluga 7, Poland.

Certain archives in Poland will actually conduct a thorough genealogical search for you. The fee is quite reasonable. For further information, write to Narodowy Bank Polski, V Oddzial Miejski, 1052-882 rachunek srodkow specjalnych, typ 33, Naczelna Dyrekcja Archiwow Panstwowych, Warszaw, ul. Dluga 6, Poland.

The LDS library in Utah also has copies of many documents found in the archives of Poland. For any other genealogical questions, you might want to contact Dyr. Hieronim Kubiak, Uniwersytet Jagiellonski, Instytut Badan Polonijnych, ul. Straszewskiego 27, 31-101 Krakow, Poland.

Portugal

The genealogical records of Portugal are very similar to those of Spain. Vital records were maintained by local parishes from the mid-16th century onward, but these records have never been transferred to any major archives. As a result, you should contact the Central Archives (Arquivo dos Registos Paroquiais) at Rua dos Prazeres 41-r/c, Lisbon, 2, Portugal, and request information on tracking down church records from the town in which your ancestor lived.

The registration of vital events by civil authorities commenced in 1878, and these records are located in the offices of local officials. The Central Archives can also help you find these records.

146

There is a National Archives of Portugal (Arquivo Nacional da Torre do Tombo) which contains many useful records, such as probate documents, tax rolls, and some church records. Contact the Portuguese consul for the address.

Scotland

Since Scottish history has been ripe with conflict and warfare, it was very difficult for the Scots to maintain local archives. As a result, most records are located in central archives and are fairly easily tracked down!

For records of vital events, you should write to The Registrar General, New Register House, Princes Street, Edinburgh, EH1 3YT. Scotland has kept impeccable records of vital events since the mid-1800s, so the staff at the Registrar General should be able to find the information you need. There is a reasonable fee for their search. Incidentally, before writing to Scotland, you might want to inquire at the LDS library in Utah, as their collection of Scottish vital records is quite extensive.

For probate records of land sales that date later than the early-1600s, you should contact The Scottish Record Office, H.M. Register House, Princes Street, Edinburgh, EH1 3YX, Scotland. For other probate records, inquire at the New Register House.

The Church of Scotland (also known as the Kirk of Scotland) is the Presbyterian church. Local parishes have maintained meticulous records of baptisms since the early-1600s. If you are unable to track down your ancestor's specific parish, then you can try at the New Register House, but many of their copies of church records have yet to be indexed and ordered. Local parishes also have records called Kirk Session Papers, which document a family's move from one parish to another (or even to the New World).

Census records from the years 1841 through 1891 are available at the New Register House.

You should be aware that as well as coming to America (specifically New York, Virginia, and North and South Carolina), many Scots moved to Prince Edward Island and Nova Scotia in Canada. If you do some research in these provinces, you might find family members of whom you were previously unaware.

Spain

Spain is the home of the oldest record in Europe of genealogical value: a parish record that dates back to the year 1394! From 1570 until 1870 the Spanish Catholic church was responsible for maintaining all vital records on a parish-by-parish basis, and there are some 19,000 parishes in all! Therefore, it is essential that any genealogist studying the records of Spain familiarize himself with the 14 volume *The Guidebook of the Spanish Church*, which is an extraordinary index of all the information that the church documented. A good genealogical library, such as the LDS library in Utah, should be able to provide you with a copy.

When civil registration replaced the church's recording of vital events, the civil authorities decided to divide up registration on the basis of communities. Therefore, in order to track down your ancestor's records, you will have to contact the registrar of the town in which your ancestor lived.

There are also four national archives in Spain, each one housing different documents:

1) The Archives of the Indies in Seville has 14-million records of the military's expeditions to the American continent.

2) The National Historical Archives in Madrid has more genealogical information than any of the other three archives, as most of the records document several generations of ancestors. It also houses documents from the Inquisition, which could prove helpful in tracing your roots if you are not of Catholic descent.

3) The Archives of the Crown of Aragon in Barcelona houses the oldest church documents available to the public.

4) The Archives of Simancas in Valladolid houses military, royal, judicial, and tax records, all of which can be very useful when piecing together your family tree.

The addresses for these archives can be obtained by contacting the Spanish consul.

Sweden

Finding your roots in a Scandinavian country like Sweden can be both a joy and a pain in the neck. It is a joy due to the fact that meticulous vital records have been kept since the 17th century. It is a pain in the neck for two reasons. First, most documents recorded before the 1870s used a Gothic script that you must learn to read. And second, due to patronymics, there are very few surnames in the country (and therefore more chance for you to pursue a wrong lead). As I explained in chapter four, patronymics is a naming system in which a child's surname is a variation on the father's *first* name. For example, If Paul Johnson has a son named Mark, then Mark's surname is *Paulson*. If Mark Paulson then has a son named Richard, Richard's surname is Markson. This system is a bit confusing at first, but with a little practice you will get used to it. You should be aware that patronymics was phased out in Sweden around the turn of the 19th century.

Probate and property records from as far back as the early-1700s can be found in The Cameral Archives (*Kamararkivet*), Fack, Fyrverkarbacken 13-17, S-100 26 Stockholm, Sweden. Such probate records often include complete lists of property, descriptions of how such property was distributed after death, names and addresses of heirs, etc.

In 1867, the Swedish government started keeping accurate immigration records for all citizens moving to America. This incredibly useful information can be found at Goteborg *Landsarkivet*, The Emigrantinstitutet, P.O. Box 201, S-351 04 Vaxjo, Sweden. These records can also be found at The *Emigrantregistret*, P.O. Box 331, S: a Kyrkogatan 4, S-651 05 Karlstad, Sweden. Moreover, some lists of immigrants are on record at the LDS library in Utah.

Since the end of the 17th century, maintaining vital records in Sweden has been the duty of parish ministers. Along with vital records, they also kept household rolls (*husforhorslangder*, census-like surveys of all households) and documents about movements from one parish to another. The household rolls contain a wealth of genealogical information on everyone in the household. Records less than 100 years old generally stay in the parish, but older documents are sent to city and regional archives. The following are the addresses of these archives, along with the areas they serve:

1) For Blekinge, Kristianstad, Malmohus, and Halland: *Landsarkivet*, Fack 2016, S-220 02 Lund, Sweden.

2) For Gotland: *Landsarkivet*, P.O. Box 142, S-621 00 Visby, Sweden.

3) For Stockholm, Uppsala, Sodermanland, Orebro, Vastmanland, and Kopparberg: *Landsarkivet*, S-751 04 Uppsala, Sweden.

4) For Gavleborg, Vasternorrland, Vasterbotten, and Norrbotten: *Landsarkivet*, Nybrogatan 17, S-871 01 Harnosand, Sweden.

5) For Ostergotland, Jonkoping, Kronoberg, and Kalmar: *Landsarkivet*, S-592 00 Vadstena, Sweden.

6) For Goteborg and Bohus, Alvsborg, Skaraborg, and Varmland: *Landsarkivet*, P.O. Box 3009, Geijersgatan 1, S-400 Goteborg, Sweden.

7) For Jamtland: *Landsarkivet*, S-831 01 Ostersund, Sweden.

8) For the city of Malmo: *Stadsarkivet*, St. Petrigangen 7A, S-211 22 Malmo, Sweden.

9) For the city of Orebro: *Stadsarkivet*, Fack, S-701 01 Orebro, Sweden.

10) For the city of Stockholm: *Stadsarkivet*, P.O. Box 22063, Kungsklippan 6, S-104 22 Stockholm, Sweden.

11) For the city of Gavle: *Stadsarkivet*, Gavle centralarkiv, Stapeltorgsgatan 5B, S-802 24 Gavle, Sweden.

12) For the city of Vasteras: *Stadsarkivet*, S-721 87 Vasteras, Sweden.

13) For the city of Karlstad: *Stadsarkivet*, Stadshuset, Drottninggatan 32, S-652 25 Karlstad, Sweden.

14) For the city of Boras: *Stadsarkivet*, P.O. Box 851, S-501 15 Boras, Sweden.

15) For the city of Uppsala: *Stadsarkivet*, Uppsala kommun, P.O. Box 216, S-751 04 Uppsala, Sweden.

16) For the city of Eskilstuna: *Stadsarkivet*, Kriebsensgatan 4, S-632 00 Eskilstuna, Sweden.

17) For the city of Norrkoping: *Stadsarkivet*, Norrkopings kommun, Stadsarkivet, S-601 81 Norrkoping, Sweden.

Finally, the Royal Ministry for Foreign Affairs publishes a helpful guide called *Finding Your Forefathers: Some Hints for Americans of Swedish Origin*. This guide can be yours by writing to The Royal Ministry for Foreign Affairs, Press and Information Service, Stockholm, Sweden.

Switzerland

Switzerland has citizenship laws unlike those of any other country. An individual is a citizen of a city or town. Due to this citizenship, an individual is also a citizen of a state (canton), and national citizenship is derived from this citizenship. The maintenance of records has traditionally been divided up on the basis of cantons, regardless of whether these records were prepared by the clergy (before 1876) or by civil authorities (after 1876). Vital records are always maintained on the city or town level, so your ancestor's vital documents will be located in the town of his birth even if he moved away during his lifetime. Knowing this town, therefore, is at the heart of successfully tracing your roots in Switzerland.

Tracing genealogies in Switzerland is amazingly simple due to the foresight of the earliest citizens of that country. They instilled in their descendants a pride in their heritage that has resulted in some of the best records ever kept. If you are aware of the town in which your ancestor was born or lived, you can contact the civil registrar and ask him to prepare a family record that dates back to 1876! If you want to find records older than that, then you will need to contact the National Archives so that they can direct you to the right church archives. Their address is The National Archives, Archivstrasse 4, 3003 Bern, Switzerland.

If you do not know the town in which your ancestor was born or lived, you should look through *The Family Name Book of Switzerland*, which will show you how to trace the town through your ancestor's surname. This book is readily available at such genealogical libraries as the LDS library in Utah.

Wales

The records from Wales have been overseen by the government of England since the early 1500s. As a result, if your ancestor came from Wales, you should follow all of the procedures outlined in the previous section on England. Once again, it is best to try contacting local parishes directly, but if you are unaware of the correct parish, then you can try to find the information you need through the Society of Genealogists.

Yugoslavia

Due to the current fighting that is tearing apart the region that used to be Yugoslavia, it is unlikely that you will be able to commence any genealogical research there for some time. Each region is populated by a different cultural/religious group. Therefore, if you are aware of your ancestor's religion, then you can easily figure out which region he came from and solicit any church or civil records from that area. Conversely, if you know which region he came from, then you can deduce his religion quite simply.

Until 1946, church records were the most appropriate way of recording vital events. After 1946, civil authorities began documenting such vital events. Each region has its own archive, in which you should be able to find any of these civil documents. The addresses of these archives follow:

1) For Voivodina: *Istorijski arhiv AP Vojvodine*, Stremski Karlovci, Trga Branka Radicevica 8.

153

2) For Slovenia: *Arhiv Slovenije*, Ljubljana, levsikov trg 3.

3) For Croatia: *Arhiv Jrvatske*, Zagreb Marulicev trag 21.

4) For Bosnia: *Arhiv Bosne I Hercegovine*, Sarajevo, Save Kovacevica 6.

5) For Kosovo-Metohija: *Pikrajinski drzavni arhiv*, Pristina, Nikola Tedko 43.

6) For Serbia: *Arhiv Srbije*, Beograd, Karnedzijeva 2.

7) For Macedonia: *Arhiv Makedonije*, Skopje.

8) For Montenegro: *Arhiv SR Crne gore*, Cetinje, Totov trg.

USSR

Finding your roots in the various republics that once formed the USSR is no easy task. Many of the republics are still engulfed by sporadic warfare, and due to ever-changing borders it is sometimes difficult to know exactly which country to approach in your genealogical search.

Early in the 18th century, local parishes began keeping vital records for all members of the community. But when the new Soviet government came into power in 1918, the various religious organizations were stripped of their power. It was at this point that civil registration of vital events began. The church records are currently located in regional archives. Civil records can be found in local registrars offices.

The U.S. Department of State can help you try to find your roots in the area that used to be the USSR. Simply write to The Consular Section, American Embassy-Moscow, c/o Department of State, Washington, D.C. 20521. Be sure to ask for the order forms for public records in Russia. It can take an entire year to obtain the records you desire.

154

The Russian Historical and Genealogical Society and the Russian Nobility Association (both of which are located at 971 First Ave, New York, NY 10022), can also be of assistance to you in your search.

Ethnic Groups

African-Americans

African-Americans undoubtedly experience the most difficulty in tracing their ancestors. Many slaves had the foresight to memorize their genealogies, as was the African custom; therefore, if any of your living relatives knows your family oral history by heart, you should definitely commit it to paper as soon as possible. Using this information, you must then try to piece together the fragments of knowledge you can glean from censuses and other records already mentioned in this book.

In order to make the leap from America to finding your ancestor's village in Africa, you will have to scrutinize your oral history very closely. Listen to the sounds of places and names. If you look on a map of Africa, you will see that each region has very distinctive sounding names. If you are willing to learn a little about some of the languages of Western Africa, then this will help you differentiate the names of places and people from each region. You might then be able to associate the names of your ancestors with a certain area, or even with a particular village.

You should not undertake any attempts to trace your heritage without first reading Alex Haley's *Roots*. This wonderful book explains in depth the methods that Mr. Haley used to make connections between oral histories and written documents, enabling him to return to the village of his ancestors.

The following are the addresses for the embassies of eight West African countries that can help you with your search:

1) Office of the Embassy of Sierra Leone, 1701 19th St., Washington, D.C. 20009.

2) Office of the Embassy of Liberia, 5201 16th St., Washington, D.C. 20011.

3) Office of the Embassy of Ghana, 2460 16th St., Washington, D.C. 20009.

4) Office of the Embassy of the Ivory Coast, 2424 Massachusetts Ave, Washington, D.C. 20008.

5) Office of the Embassy of Senegal, 2121 Wyoming Ave, Washington, D.C. 20008.

6) Office of the Embassy of Togo, 2208 Massachusetts Ave, Washington, D.C. 20008.

7) Office of the Embassy of Guinea, 2112 Leroy Pl., Washington, D.C. 20008.

8) Office of the Consulate General of the Gambia, 300 East 56th St., New York, NY 10018.

Jewish Ancestors

Due to the Holocaust, many Jews face a seemingly insurmountable task in piecing together their genealogies. But this is not necessarily the case. In fact, thanks to a recent resurgence in interest, many Jewish genealogical societies are forming, and they can be of great help to you while searching for your roots. Everyday more "lost" records are found, some over 500 years old!

The following are the addresses of some of the societies that can assist you:

1) The American Jewish Historical Society, Two Thornton Rd, Watham, Massachusetts 02154.

2) The Diaspora Research Institute, Tel Aviv University, Ramat-Aviv, Israel.

3) Institute for Contemporary Jewry, The Hebrew University, Givat Ram, Jerusalem, Israel.

4) Ben-Zvi Institute for Research on Jewish Communities in the East, The Hebrew University, Givat Ram, Jerusalem, Israel.

The LDS library in Utah also has an extensive collection of records on Jewish Ancestry.

Native Americans

The National Archives and their respective branches (particularly the Federal Archives and Records Center at P.O. Box 6216 in Fort Worth, Texas) have a great deal of Native American records in their files. Among the tribal records you should research are:

- Indian Census Rolls, 1885-1940
- Removal records, 1815-1850
- Tribal enrollment records, 1827-present
- 1832 Census of the Creek Nation
- 1835 Census of the Cherokee Nation
- Land allotment records, 1856-1935
- Probate records, 1906-present
- United States censuses from 1860 onwards
- Annuity rolls, 1850-1887

If you reach a dead end at the National Archives, try writing to the Bureau of Indian Affairs, 1951 Constitution Avenue NW, Washington, DC 20245. They will provide you with the name and location of the agency responsible for the tribe to which your ancestor belonged.

11

SHARING YOUR FAMILY HISTORY WITH YOUR RELATIVES

Writing Up Your Family History

By the time you are ready to write up your family history, you will probably be extremely familiar with the correct formats for genealogical records and histories. However, there are still several things you can do to turn your family history into an exciting piece of literature as opposed to a dry, stodgy document.

First of all, never forget to put some kind of a cover on your family history. This is a record that will be preserved for generations, so you want it to be as polished as possible. When your family holds reunions decades (or even centuries) in the future, you will want your descendants to look through the pages of a volume that has a beautiful cover on it. The cover should contain something reflective of the family; a coat of arms, an old portrait of one of your ancestors or their home, an old family photograph, or a map detailing the travels of your original ancestors all make outstanding front covers.

The first page of the book should be the title page, indicating the name of the family who is the subject of the history. You might also want to indicate that you were the person who researched and prepared the history—don't be ashamed to take credit where credit is due.

Place as many charts, photographs, and maps as possible in the book. A picture really does say a thousand words, and the readers of your family history will want to *see* as many of your ancestors as possible. They will want to see these pictures so that they can *feel* what the lives of your ancestors must have been like, and therefore have a better understanding of the past. Did your ancestors live in plush New England towns, or did they work on grueling pioneer ranches? A photograph will document this better than words ever could.

Begin with the first progenitor (or emigrant ancestor). The first paragraph should contain the dates of his birth and death, parentage, and a reference as to where this information came from. Never forget to include references in any part of your family history, as other genealogists reading your history may want to refer to the sources that you used. The best genealogies contain pages of endnotes (which are just like footnotes, except that they all appear at the end of the record) and a bibliography page. Endnotes contain the name of the author, the name of the book (or any other type of document you used), the name and address of the publisher (if applicable), the date of publication, the edition, and the page number. The data in the bibliography should be very similar, except that no page numbers should be given, and the books should be arranged alphabetically by the author's surname.

The next paragraph should refer to the progenitor's marriage, including date and place, the wife's full name, parentage, and dates of birth and death. If she was a widow, then the names of all previous husbands should be given. Don't be afraid to get a little creative when preparing your family history; if possible, tell the reader whether they had a loving or distant marriage. Personal information is what makes a genealogy pleasurable and memorable, not facts and figures. Give a separate paragraph to each of the progenitor's marriages, if he had more than one.

The following paragraph should include a brief description of his life and accomplishments, including military duties, any offices or professions held, where he lived, etc. This is where it really gets exciting! Tell your readers about all of the battles he fought in as a soldier, about all of the incredible things he accomplished during his lifetime. This is your chance to paint a rich and textured portrait of the past.

The next paragraph should be the abstract of both his and his wife's will. Define all relations between heirs and the first progenitor. Include the date of the will and probate. This paragraph gives you even more opportunities to describe in wonderful detail the life of your ancestor; was there, for example, some kind of a feud which resulted in his second son being written out of the will?

Next will come the names of any children.

At the end of the summary, there should be the endnote page of any and all references used in gathering the above material.

The next biographical sketch will be that of the eldest son, followed by each successive son or daughter.

Assign the progenitor the numeral 1. Each of his children should receive a lowercase Roman numeral, such as i, ii, iii, etc. Whenever a son goes on to become the head of a family unit, he should also receive a number of his own, making sure that the numbers are kept in consecutive order from the oldest to the youngest.

You should also write a brief introduction which acknowledges any and all who helped you during your search, a few interesting anecdotes about problems and surprises you ran into while conducting your search, and any explanatory material regarding your numbering system, endnotes, and the like.

Your family history should also contain an index of all names and place names, so that other genealogists can easily find the information that they need.

Many people who compile their family histories only make a dozen or so copies to give to their relatives. But I highly urge you to actually publish your history and send copies to as many genealogical libraries and booksellers as possible. Remember how difficult it was to find the information you needed? Don't you want to make it easier for future genealogists to complete their searches? The information found in your history might be of vital importance for another genealogist to piece together his or her own history.

Publishing a family history is actually quite easy, as there is such a high demand for them. All of the genealogical journals already mentioned in this book accept unsolicited histories, and the Genealogy Club of America can even help you get it published in book form!

Celebrating Your Success with a Family Reunion

Bringing together your extended family should be looked upon as the ultimate goal of your search for your family roots. In today's hectic age, when so many of our country's traditional values seem to be falling by the wayside, keeping a strong sense of your family's heritage is more important than ever. Children in particular relish the comfort and security that comes along with a sense of family history, of generation succeeding generation, and of carrying on the honor and tradition of the family name.

The best way to go about getting together your newfound family is to plan a reunion over a holiday weekend. Pick a location in a region of the country that is somewhat central to where the majority of your family members live. If possible, try to choose a spot that is in some way relevant to the history of your family—perhaps the city where one of the family's oldest ancestors lived.

You should have plenty of copies of the material you have collected during your search available for everyone to see, including family group charts, photographs, newspaper clippings, diaries, birth, marriage, and death certificates, and the like. If you can afford the expense, the ideal gift for all of your relatives would be a copy of your published family history. It would also be wise to bring along a tape recorder and either a still camera or a video camera so that you will be able to record the events that take place over the weekend, including all of the valuable stories that will surely be told by family members about themselves and their ancestors.

12

BIBLIOGRAPHY

Bibliography

Allcock, Hubert. *Heraldic Design*. New York: Tudor Publishing Co., 1962.

Andereck, Paul A., and Richard A. Pence. *Computer Genealogy: A Guide to Research Through High Technology*. Salt Lake City: 1985.

Arthur, Stephen, and Julia Arthur. *Your Life and Times: How to Put a Life Story on Tape. An Oral Handbook*. Baltimore: 1987.

Askin, Jayne, with Bob Oskam. *Search: A Handbook for Adoptees and Birth Parents*. New York: 1982.

"Availability of Federal Mortality Census Schedules, 1850-1885." In *National Genealogical Society Quarterly 52*, Dec. 1964.

"Availability of Names Indexes to Federal Population Census Schedules, 1790-1890." In *National Genealogical Society Quarterly 51*, Sept. 1963.

Babbel, June Andrew, comp. *Lest We Forget: A Guide to Genealogical Research in the Nation's Capital*, 3rd ed. Annendale, VA: Potomac State of the Curch of Jesus Christ of Latter-day Saints, 1969.

Bailey, Thomas A. *The American Spirit: United States History as Seen by Contemporaries*, vol. 1. Boston: D.C. Heath & Co., 1963.

Banaka, William H. *Training in Depth Interviewing*. New York: Harper & Row, Publishers, 1971.

Barck, Oscar, Theodore, Jr., and Hugh Talmage Lefler. *Colonial America*. New York: The Macmillan Co., 1958.

Bardsley, Charles Waring. *A Dictionary of English and Welsh Surnames with Special American Instances*. London, 1901.

Barron, Arthur Oswald. "Heraldry." In *Shakespeare's England*. Oxford: Clarendon Press, 1916.

Baxter, Angus. *In Search of Your European Roots*. Baltimore: 1988.

Beard, Timothy Field, with Denise Demong. *How to Find Your Family Roots*. New York: 1977.

Benes, Josef. *O ceskych prijmenich*. Prague: Naki. Ceskoslovenske Akademie ved, 1962.

Bentley, Elizabeth Petty. *County Courthouse Book*. Baltimore: 1990.

Berry, Ellen Thomas, and David Allen Berry. *Our Quaker Ancestors: Finding Them in Quaker Records*. Baltimore: 1987.

Black, Dr. George F. *The Surnames of Scotland, Their Origin, Meaning, and History*. New York: New York Public Library, 1968.

Blassingame, John. *Slave Testimony: Two Centuries of Letters, Speeches, Interviews, and Autobiographies*. Baton Rouge: Louisiana State University Press, 1977.

Blockson, Charles L., and Ron Fry. *Black Genealogy*. Englewood Cliffs, NJ: Prentice-Hall, 1977.

Blum, John M., et al. *The National Experience: A History of the United States*, 2nd ed. New York: Harcourt, Brace & World, 1968.

Boutell, Charles. *Boutell's Heraldry*, 5th ed. C.W. Scott-Giles and J.P. Brooke-Little, eds. London: Warne, 1966.

Bradford, Thomas C. *The Bibliographer's Manual of American History, Containing an Account of All States, Territories, Towns, and County Histories...With Verbatim Copies of the Titles, and Useful Bibliographical Notes*. Stan V. Henkels, ed. 5 vols. Detroit: Gale Research, 1968.

Bragrow, Leo. *History of Cartography*, R.A. Skelton, ed. Cambridge, MA: Harvard University Press, 1964.

Burke, John Bernard. *The General Armory of England, Scotland, Ireland, and Wales*. London: Harrison, 1878.

Camp, Anthony J. *Everyone Has Roots: An Introduction to English Genealogy*. Baltimore, MD: Genealogical Publishing Co., 1978.

Camp, Anthony J. *Tracing Your Ancestors in England*. Baltimore, MD: Genealogical Publishing Co., 1975.

Camp, Anthony J. *Wills and Their Whereabouts*. London: 1974.

Carter, Clarence E., Sr. "The Territorial Papers as a Source for the Genealogist." In *National Genealogical Society Quarterly 37*, Dec. 1949.

Cerny, Johni, and Arlene Eakle. *Ancestry's Guide to Research: Case Studies in American Genealogy*. Salt Lake City: 1985.

Cerny, Johni, and Wendy Elliot. *The Library: A Guide to the LDS Family History Library*. Salt Lake City: 1988.

Chapuy, Paul. *Origine des Noms Patronymiques Francais*. Paris: 1934.

Child, Heather. *Heraldic Design: A Handbook for Students*. London: G. Bell, 1965.

Child, Sargent B., and D.P. Holmes. *A Bibliography of Research Projects Reports. Checklist of Historical Records Survey Publications, Technical Series, Research and Records Bibliographies, 7*. Washington, DC: 1943.

Chuks-Orji, Ogonna. *Names from Africa, Their Origin, Meaning, and Pronunciation*. New York: Johnson Publishing Co., 1972.

Colket, Meredith B., Jr., and Frank E. Bridgers. *Guide to Genealogical Records in the National Archives*. National Archives Publication No. 64-8. Washington, DC: National Archives and Records Service, 1964.

Crowther, George R., III. *Surname Index to Sixty-five Volumes of Colonial and Revolutionary Pedigrees*. National Genealogical Society special publication 27. Washington, DC: The Society, 1964.

d'Angerville, Count Howard H. *Living Descendents of Blood Royal* (4 vols.). London: 1971.

Daniel, J.R.V. *A Handbook of Virginia History.* Richmond: The Virginia Department of Conservation and Development, 1949.

Dauzat, Albert. *Dictionnaire Etymologique des Noms de Famille et Prenoms de France.* Paris: 1951.

Dennys, Rodney. *The Heraldic Imagination.* New York: Crown Publishers, 1976.

De Platt, Lyman. *Genealogical and Historical Guide to Latin America.* Detroit: 1978.

Doane, Gilbert H. *Searching For Your Ancestors,* 2nd ed. Minneapolis: University of Minnesota Press, 1952.

Everton, George B., ed. *The Handy Book for Genealogists.* Logan, UT: Everton Publishers, 1971.

Fairbairn, James. *Crests of the Families of Great Britain*, 4th ed. 2 vols. London: Jack, 1905.

Fairchild, Henry Pratt. *Immigration.* New York: Macmillan Publishing Co., 1913.

Falley, Margaret Dickson. *Irish and Scotch-Irish Ancestral Research: A Guide to the Genealogical Records, Methods and Sources in Ireland.* Evanston, IL: 1962.

Filby, P. William, comp. *American and British Genealogy and Heraldry, a Selected list of Books.* Chicago: American Library Assoc., 1970.

Filby, P. William, ed. *Passenger Lists Bibliography,* Detroit, MI: 1988.

Fletcher, William. *Recording Your Family History: A Guide to Preserving Oral History and Using Audio and Video Tape.* Berkeley: 1990.

Fox-Davies, A.C. *A Complete Guide to Heraldry.* London: Thomas Nelson and Sons, Ltd., 1969.

Franklin, W. Neil. "Availability of Federal Population Census Schedules in the States." In *National Genealogical Society Quarterly 50,* Mar. and Jun. 1962.

Fucilla, Joseph Guerin. *Our Italian Surnames*. Evanston: 1949.

Gardner, David E., and Frank Smith. *Genealogical Research in England and Wales*. Salt Lake City: Bookcraft, 1964.

Gayre, Robert. *Heraldic Standards and Other Ensigns*. Edinburgh, Scotland: Oliver and Boyd, 1959.

Gottschald, Max. *Deutsche Namenkunde*. Berlin: Dritte Vermehrte Auslage, 1954.

Greenwood, Val D. *The Researcher's Guide to American Genealogy*. Baltimore: Genealogical Publishing Co., 1973.

Groene, Bertram Hawthorne. *Tracing Your Civil War Ancestor*. Winston-Salem, NC: 1973.

Hale, Richard W. *Guide to Photocopied Historical Materials in the United States and Canada*. Ithaca: Cornell University Press for the American Historical Association, 1961.

Hamer, Philip M. *A Guide to Archives and Manuscripts in the United States*. New Haven: Yale University Press, 1961.

Hamilton-Edwards, G.K.S. *In Search of British Ancestry*, 4th ed. Baltimore: 1983.

Hansen, Marcus Lee. *The Atlantic Migration, 1607-1860*. Cambridge: Harvard University Press, 1951.

Hassall, W.O. *History Through Surnames*. Oxford, England: Pergamon Press, 1967.

Hawke, David. *The Colonial Experience*. New York: Bobbs-Merrill Co., 1966.

Helmbold, F. Wilbur. *Guide to Researching Your Family History*. Birmingham, AL: 1976.

Hill, Roscoe R. *Los Archivos Nacionales de la America Latina*. Havana: 1948.

Hilton, Suzanne. *Who do You Think You Are? Digging for Your Family Roots*. Philadelphia: Westminster Press, 1977.

Hook, J.N. *Family Names: How Our Surnames Came to America*, New York: 1982.

Innes, Thomas, of Learney. *Scots Heraldry: A Handbook on the Historical Principles and Modern Applications of the Art and Science*, 2nd ed. Edinburgh, Scotland: Oliver and Boyd, 1956.

Jacobus, Donald Lines. *Genealogy as Pastime and Profession*. Baltimore: Genealogical Publishing Co., 1968.

Jarboe, Betty M. *Obituaries: A Guide to Sources*, 2nd ed. Boston: 1989.

Jonasson, Eric. *Tracing Your Icelandic Family Tree*. Winnipeg, Manitoba: 1978.

Jones, Maldwyn Allen. *American Immigration*. Chicago: University of Chicago Press, 1967.

Kaminkow, Marion, and Jack Kaminkow. *Original Lists of Emigrants in Bondage from London to the American Colonies, 1719-1744*. Baltimore: Magna Carta Book Co., 1967.

Karp, Abraham. *Golden Door to America: The Jewish Immigrant Experience*. New York: Viking Press, 1976.

Kazanoff, Benzion C. *A Dictionary of Jewish Names and their History*. New York: Schocken Books, 1977.

Kennedy, John F. *A Nation of Immigrants*. New York: Harper & Row, 1964.

Kephart, Calvin. *Origin of Herladry in Europe*, 3rd ed. Baltimore: Heraldic Book Co., 1964.

Kirkham, E. Kay. *A Survey of American Church Records*. Logan, UT: Everton Publishers, 1971.

Kirkham, E. Kay. *A Survey of American Census Schedules; an Explanation and Description of our Federal Census Enumerations 1790 to 1950*. Salt Lake City: Deseret Book Co., 1959.

Kirkham, E. Kay. *The Counties of The United States and their Genealogical Value*. Salt Lake City: Deseret Book Co., 1975.

Kirkham, E. Kay. *The Land Records of America and their Genealogical Value*. Salt Lake City: Deseret Book Co., 1964.

Kirkham, E. Kay. *Some of the Military Records of America Before 1900: Their Use and Value in Genealogical and Historical Research*. Salt Lake City: Deseret Book Co., 1964.

Kirkham, E. Kay. *How to Read the Handwriting and Records of Early America*, 2nd ed. Salt Lake City: Deseret Book Co., 1964.

Kirkham, E. Kay. *Simplified Genealogy for Americans*. Salt Lake City: Deseret Book Co., 1968.

Kurzweil, Arthur. *From Generation to Generation: How to Trace Your Jewish Genealogy and Personal History*. New York: 1980.

Library of Congress. Map Division. *A List of Geographical Atlases in the Library of Congress*. Vol. 1—, 1909—. New York: Paladin Press, 1968.

Lichtman, Allen J. *Your Family History: How to Use Oral History, Personal Family Archives, and Public Documents to Discover Your Heritage*. New York: 1978.

Linder, Bill R. *How to Trace Your Family Tree*. New York: 1978.

Lister, Raymond. *Antique Maps and Cartographers*. Hamden, CT: Shoe String Press, 1970.

MacLysaght, Edward. *A Guide to Irish Surnames*. Dublin: 1964.

Maduell, Charles R. *The Romance of Spanish Surnames*. New Orleans: 1967.

Mann, Thomas Clifford, and Janet Greene. *Over their Dead Bodies: Yankee Epitaphs and History*. Battleboro, VT: Stephen Green Press, 1962.

Marzio, Peter C., ed. *A Nation of Nations*. New York: Harper & Row Publishers, 1976.

Matthews, Constance M. *English Surnames*. New York: Charles Scribenr's Sons, 1967.

Matthews, William, et al. *American Diaries...an Annotated Bibliography of American Diaries Written Prior to 1861*. Boston: Canner, 1959.

Meyer, Mary K., ed. *Meyer's Directory of Genealogical Societies in the U.S.A. and Canada*, 8th ed. Mt. Airy, MD: 1990.

Mitchell, Brian. *A Guide to Irish Parish Registers*. Baltimore: 1988.

Mitler, Olga. *Genealogical Research for Czech and Slovak Americans*. Detroit: 1978.

Moncreiffe, Iain, and Don Pottinger. *Simple Heraldry*. Edinburgh, Scotland: Nelson Press, 1953.

Moody, David. *Scottish Family History*. Baltimore: 1990.

Moulton, Joy Wade. *Genealogical Resources in English Repositories*. Columbus, OH: 1988.

Neagles, James C. *Confederate Research Sources: A Guide to Archive Collections*. Salt Lake City: 1986.

Neagles, James C. and Lila L. Neagles. *Locating Your Immigrant Ancestor: A Guide to Naturalization Records*. Logan, UT: 1986.

Neubecker, Ottfried. *Heraldry Sources, Symbols, and Meanings*. New York: McGraw-Hill Books Co., 1976.

Newman, John J. *American Naturalization Process and Procedures, 1790-1985*. Indianapolis: 1985.

Nielson, Paul Anton. *Swiss Genealogical Research: An Introductory Guide*. Virginia Beach, VA: 1979.

Papworth, John W., and Alfred W. Morant. *An Alphabetical Dictionary of Coats of Arms...Ordinary of British Armorials*. London, England: Tabard Publications, 1961.

Parker, James. *A Glossary of Terms Used in Heraldry*. Rutland, VT: Charles E. Tuttle Co., 1970.

Paul, James B. *Ordinary of Scottish Arms*. Edinburgh, Scotland: Green, 1903.

Pine, Leslie Gilbert. *Desecendants of Norman Ancestry*. Rutland, VT: Charles E. Tuttle Co., 1973.

Pine, Leslie Gilbert. *The Story of Surnames*. Aylesbury, Bucks, England: Hazel Watson & Viney, 1965.

Pine, Leslie Gilbert. *International Heraldry*. Rutland, VT: Charles E. Tuttle Co., 1970.

Puttock, A.G. *A Dictionary of Heraldry and Related Subjects*. Baltimore: Genealogical Publishing Co., 1970.

Reaney, Dr. P. H. *Dictionary of British Surnames*. England: 1958.

Rider, Fremont J., ed. *American Genealogical-Biographical Index*, Middletown, CT: 1952—.

Riestap, J.B. *Armorial General*, 2nd ed. London, England: Heraldry Today, 1965.

Rillera, Mary Jo. *The Adoption Searchbook*, 2nd ed. Logan, UT: 1985.

Rose, James, and Alice Eicholz. *Black Genesis*. Detroit: 1978.

Rottenberg, Dan. *Finding our Fathers: A Guidebook to Jewish Genealogy*. New York: Random House, 1977.

Ryan, James G. *Irish Records: Sources for Family and Local History*. Salt Lake City: 1988.

Ryskamp, George R. *Tracing Your Hispanic Heritage*. Riverside, CA: 1984.

Sack, SallyAnn Amdur. *A Guide to Jewish Genealogical Research in Israel.* Baltimore: 1987.

Schlesinger, Arthur M. *Paths to the Present.* New York: Macmillan Publishing Co., 1949.

Schlyter, Daniel M. *A Handbook of Czechoslovak Genealogical Research.* Buffalo Grove, IL: 1985.

Schweitzer, George K. *Revolutionary War Genealogy.* Knoxville, TN: 1982.

Shumway, Gary L., and William G. Hartley. *An Oral History Primer.* Salt Lake City: Deseret Book Co., 1974.

Smith, Eldon C. *American Surnames,* Baltimore: MD, 1986.

Smith, Elsdon Coles. *Dictionary of American Family Names.* New York: 1956.

Smith, Elsdon Coles. *Story of Our Names.* New York: Harper & Brothers, 1950.

Stephenson, Jean. *Heraldry for the American Genealogist.* Special publication no. 25. Washington, DC: National Genealogical Society, 1959.

Stephenson, Richard W. *Land Ownership Maps: A Checklist of Nineteenth Century United States County Maps in the Library of Congress.* Washington, DC: Superintendant of Documents, 1967.

Streets, David H. *Slave Genealogy: A Research Guide with Case Studies.* Bowie, MD: 1986.

Stryker-Rodda, Kenn, ed. *Genealogical Research,* vol. 2. Washington, DC: American Society of Genealogists, 1971.

Sturm, Duane, and Pat Sturm. *Video Family History.* Salt Lake City: 1989.

Tibon, Gutierre. *Onomastica Hispano Americana.* Mexico: 1961.

Unbegaun, Boris O. *Russian Surnames.* Oxford: Clarendon Press, 1972.

United States Local Histories in the Library of Congress: A Bibliography. Baltimore, MD: 1975.

Waitley, Douglas. *Roads of Destiny*. Washington, DC: Robert B. Luce, 1970.

Walch, Timothy. *Our Family, Our Town: Essays on Family and Local History Sources in the National Archives*. Washington, DC: 1987.

Weitzman, David. *Underfoot: An Everyday Guide to Exploring the American Past*. New York: Charles Scribner's Sons, 1976.

Whitehill, Walter Muir. *Independent Historical Societies*. Boston: The Boston Athenaeum, 1962.

Whyte, Donald, ed. *A Dictionary of Scottish Emigrants to the U.S.A.* Baltimore, MD: Magna Carta Book Co., 1972.

Williams, Ethel W. *Know Your Ancestors*. Rutland, VT: Charles E. Tuttle Book Co., 1960.

Wright, Norman Edgar. *Building An American Ancestral: A Study in Genealogy*. Provo, UT: Brigham Young University Press, 1974.

Young, Tommie M. *African-American Genealogy: Exploring and Documenting the Black Family*. Clarksville, TN: 1980.

Yurdan, Marilyn. *Tracing Your Ancestors (British)*. Newton Abbot, England: 1988.

Zabriskie, George O. *Climbing our Family Tree Systematically*. Salt Lake City: Parliament Press, 1969.

13

APPENDIX

Libraries with Excellent Genealogical Collections

Alabama
Birmingham Public Library
2020 7th Ave
N. Birmingham, AL 35203

Alabama Genealogical Society
AGS Depository
and Headquarters
Samford University Library
800 Lakeshore Dr
Birmingham, AL 35229

University of Alabama
William Stanley Hoole
Special Collections Library
Box 870266
Tuscaloosa, AL 35487-9784

Alaska
Alaska Division
of State Libraries
Pouch G
State Capitol
Juneau, AK 99801

Alaska Historical Library
and Museum
Juneau, AK 99801

University of Alaska,
Fairbanks
Alaska and Polar Regions
Department
Elmer E. Rasmuson Library
Fairbanks, AK 99701

Arizona
Arizona and the West Library
318 University of Arizona
Tucson, AZ 85721

Arizona Historical Society
Library
949 East Second Street
Tucson, AZ 85719

Arizona State Department
of Library Archives
and Public Records
State Capital
1700 West Washington
Phoenix, AZ 85007

Flagstaff City Library
11 W Cherry Ave
Flagstaff, AZ 86001

Tucson Public Library
200 S 6th Ave
Tucson, AZ 85701

Arkansas
Arkansas State Library
One Capital Mall
Little Rock, AR 722901

Little Rock Public Library
700 Louisiana St
Little Rock, AR 72201

Pine Bluff and
Jefferson County Library
219 E 8th Ave
Pine Bluff, AR 71601

Southwest Arkansas
Regional Archives
Mary Medaris, Director
Old Washington
Historic State Park
Washington, AR 71862

California
Bancroft Library
University of California
Berkeley, CA 94720

California State Archives
Rm. 200
1020 "0" St
Sacramento, CA 95814

California State Library
California Section, Room 304
Library and Courts Building
914 Capitol Mall
Sacramento, CA 95814

California State Library
Sutro Branch
480 Winston Dr
San Francisco, CA 94132

Genealogical Research Center
Department of
Special Collections
San Francisco Public Library
480 Winston Drive
San Francisco, CA 94132

Huntington Library
San Marino, CA 91108

Long Beach Public Library
Ocean at Pacific Ave
Long Beach, CA 90802

Los Angeles Public Library
60 W Fifth St
Los Angeles, CA 90071

Oakland Public Library
14th and Oak St
Oakland, CA 94612

Pasadena Public Library
285 E Walnut
Pasadena, CA 91101

Pomona Public Library
P.O. Box 2271
Pomona, CA 91766

University of California,
Berkeley
Bancroft Library
Berkeley, CA 94720

University of California,
Los Angeles
Department of
Special Collections
University Research Library,
Floor A
Los Angeles, CA 90024-1575

Colorado
Boulder Public Library
1000 Canyon Blvd
Boulder, CO 80302

Colorado Historical Society
Stephen H. Hart Library
Colorado State
History Museum
1300 Broadway
Denver, CO 80203

Colorado Springs
Public Library
21 Kiowa St
Colorado Springs, CO 80902

Denver Public Library
1357 Broadway
Denver, CO 80203

179

Historical Society Library
14th and Sherman
Denver, CO 80203

Montrose Public Library
City Hall
Montrose, CO 81401

Norlin Library
University of Colorado
Campus Box 184
Boulder, CO 80309

Penrose Public Library
20 N Cascade
Colorado Springs, CO 80902

Stagecoach Library
1840 S. Wolcott Ct.
Denver, CO 80219

Tutt Library
Colorado College
Colorado Springs, CO 80903

Connecticut
Connecticut Historical Society
Library
1 Elizabeth Street
Hartford, CT 06105

Connecticut State Library
231 Capitol Ave
Hartford, CT 06115

Godfrey Memorial Library
134 Newfield St
Middletown, CT 06457

Hartford Public Library
500 Main St
Hartford, CT 06103

New Haven Public Library
133 Elm Street
New Haven, CT 06510

Otis Library
261 Main St
Norwich, CT 06360

Public Library
63 Huntington St
New London, CT 06320

Yale University Libraries
Box 1603A
Yale Station
New Haven, CT 06520

Delaware
Division of History
Department of State
Hall of Records
Dover, DE 19901

The Public Archives
Commission
Hall of Records
Dover, DE 19901

University Library
University of Delaware
Newark, DE 19711

District of Columbia
District of Columbia
Public Library
Washingtoniana Division
901 G Street NW
Washington, DC 20001

Genealogical Department
Library of Congress Annex
Washington, DC 20540

Library of Congress
Local History and Genealogy
Reading Room Section
Thomas Jefferson Building,
Room LJ244
101 Independence Avenue SE
Washington, DC 20540

National Archives
and Records Service
8 and Pennsylvania Ave, N.W.
Washington, DC 20408

Florida
Florida State Library
Supreme Court Bldg
Tallahassee, FL 32304

Jacksonville Public Library
122 N Ocean St
Jacksonville, FL 32202

Miami-Dade Public Library
1 Biscayne Blvd N
Miami, FL 33132
Orlando Public Library
10 N Rosalind Ave
Orlando, FL 38201

P.K. Yonge Library
of Florida History
University of Florida
Gainesville, FL 32601

Palm Beach County
Genealogical Library
Box 1746
W Palm Beach, FL 33402

State Library of Florida
R.A. Gray Bldg
Tallahassee, FL 32301

Tampa Public Library
900 N Ashley St
Tampa, FL 33602

University of Florida
P.K. Yonge Library of Florida
History
404 Library West
Gainesville, FL 32611

Georgia
Atlanta Public Library
1 Margaret Mitchell Sq
Atlanta, GA 30303

Bradley Memorial Library
Bradley Dr
Columbus, GA 31906

Brunswick Regional Library
208 Gloucester St
Brunswick, GA 31521

Carnegie Library
607 Broad St
Rome, GA 30161

Decatur-DeKalb Library
215 Sycamore St
Decatur, GA 30030

Georgia Department
of Archives and History
330 Capitol Ave
Atlanta, GA 30334

Georgia Historical Society
Library
501 Whittaker St.
Savannah, GA 31401

Georgia State Library
301 State Judicial Bldg
Capitol Hill Stn
Atlanta, GA 30334

Georgia State University
Archives
104 Decatur St SE
Atlanta, GA 30303

Genealogical Center Library
Box 71343
Marietta, GA 30007-1343

Lake Lanier Regional Library
Pike St
Lawrenceville, GA 30245

Piedmont Regional Library
Winder, GA 30680

Savannah Public Library
2002 Bull St
Savannah, GA 31401

Southwest Georgia Regional
Library
Shotwell at Monroe
Bainbridge, GA 31717

Washington Memorial Library
1180 Washington Ave
Macon, GA 31201

Hawaii
Brigham Young University
Hawaii Campus
55-220 Hulanui St
Laie, HI 96762

DAR Memorial Library
1914 Makiki Hts Dr
Honolulu, HI 96822

Library of Hawaii
King and Punchbowl Sts.
Honolulu, HI 96813

Idaho
Boise State University Library
Boise, ID 83725

Idaho Genealogical Library
325 W. State
Boise, ID 83702

Idaho State Historical Society
Library and Archives
610 North Julia Davis Drive
Boise, ID 83702

Idaho State University Library
Pocatello, ID 83209

Illinois
Chicago Historical Society
Research Collections
Clark Street at North Avenue
Chicago, IL 60614

Illinois State Archives
Archives Bldg
Springfield, IL 62706

Illinois State Historical Library
Old State Capitol
Springfield, IL 62706

Madison County
Historical Museum
and Library
715 N. Main St.
Edwardsville, IL 62025

Newberry Library
60 W Walton St
Chicago, IL 60610

Peoria Public Library
111 N Monroe St
Peoria, IL 61602

Rock Island Public Library
Rock Island, IL 61201

Rockford Public Library
215 N Wyman St
Rockford, IL 61101

University of Illinois Library
Urbana, IL 61801

Vogel Genealogical Research
Library
305 1st St
Holcomb, IL 61043

Indiana
Allen County Public Library
P.O. Box 2270
Fort Wayne, IN 46801

Public Library of Fort Wayne
Ft Wayne, IN 46802

Genealogy Division
Indiana State Library
140 N Senate St
Indianapolis, IN 46204

Iowa
Iowa Genealogical Society
Library
P.O. Box 7735
Des Moines, IA 50320

State Library of Iowa
East 12th and Grand
Des Moines, IA 50319

State Historical Society of Iowa
Library
402 Iowa Avenue
Iowa City, IA 52240

Kansas
Bethel Historical Library
Bethel College N
Newton, KS 67114

Garden City Public Library
210 N 7th
Garden City, KS 67846

Johnson County Library
8700 W 63rd St
Shawnee Mission, KS 66202

Kansas State
Historical Society Library
Historical Research Center
120 West Tenth Street
Topeka, KS 66612

Public Library
Independence, KS 67301

Public Library
6th and Minnesota St
Kansas City, KS 66101

Topeka Public Library
1515 West 10th
Topeka, KS 66604

Wichita City Library
220 S Main St
Wichita, KS 67202

Kentucky
Breckinridge County
Public Library
Hardinsburg, KY 40143

183

Kentucky Historical Society
KHS Library
Old Capital Annex
300 West Broadway
Box H
Frankfort, KY 40602-2108

Kentucky State Library
and Archives
Public Records Division
300 Coffee Tree Road
P.O. Box 537
Frankfurt, KY 40602-0537

Louisville Free Public Library
4th and York Sts.
Louisville, KY 40203

National Society of the Sons
of the American Revolution
Genealogy Library
1000 South Fourth Street
Louisville, KY 40203

Western Kentucky University
Library
Bowling Green, KY 42101

Louisiana
Hill Memorial Library
Louisiana State University
Baton Rouge, LA 70803

Howard Tilton Library
Map and Genealogy Room
Tulane University
New Orleans, LA 70118

Louisiana State Library
Box 131
Baton Rouge, LA 70821

New Orleans Public Library
219 Loyola Ave
New Orleans, LA 70140

Quachita Parish Public Library
1800 Stubbs Ave
Monroe, LA 71201

Shreve Memorial Library
424 Texas St
Shreveport, LA 71120

Tangipahoa Parish Library
Amite, LA 70422

Maine
Maine Historical Society
Library
485 Congress Street
Portland, ME 04101

Maine State Library
State House
Augusta, ME 04330

Bangor Public Library
145 Harlow St
Bangor, ME 04401

Maryland
Enoch Pratt Free Library
400 Cathedral St
Baltimore, MD 21201

George Peabody Library of the
Johns Hopkins University
17 E. Mt. Vernon Place
Baltimore, MD 21202

Hall of Records
College Ave and St. Johns St
Annapolis, MD 21401

Maryland State Library
Court of Appeals Bldg.
361 Rose Blvd.
Annapolis, MD 21401

Massachusetts
Boston Public Library
Box 286
Boston, MA 02117

Essex Institute
132 Essex St.
Salem, MA 01970

Massachusetts State Library
Beacon Hill
Boston, MA 02155

New England
Historic Genealogical Society
Library
89-101 Newbury Street
Boston, MA 02116

Secretary of the
Commonwealth
Public Documents Division
State House
Boston, MA 02133

Springfield City Library
220 State Stret
Springfield, MA 01103

Michigan
Detroit Society
for Genealogical Research
Detroit Public Library
5201 Woodward Ave
Detroit, MI 48202

Flint Public Library
1026 E Kearsley
Flint, MI 48502

Grand Rapids Public Library
111 Library St NE
Grand Rapids, MI 49502

Herrick Public Library
300 River Ave
Holland, MI 49423

Library of Michigan
717 W. Allegan
P.O. Box 30007
Lansing, MI 48909

Mason County Genealogical
and Historical Resource Center
c/o Rose Hawley Museum
305 E. Filer Street
Ludington, MI 49431

Michigan Department of
Education
State Library
Box 30007
Lansing, MI 48909

Minnesota
Folke Bernadette
Memorial Library
Gustavus Adolphus College
St. Peter, MN 56082

Minneapolis Public Library
300 Nicolet Ave
Minneapolis, MN 55401

Minnesota Historical Society
Library Reference Services
690 cedar Street
St. Paul, MN 55101

Public Library
90 W 4th
St. Paul, MN 55102

Rolvaag Memorial Library
St. Olaf College
Northfield, MN 55057

University of Minnesota
Library
Minneapolis, MN 55455

Mississippi
Attala County Library
328 Goodman St
Kosciusko, MS 39090

Biloxi Public Library
P.O. Box 467
Biloxi, MS 39533

Department of Archives
and History
Archive and History Bldg
Capitol Green
Jackson, MS 39205

Evans Memorial Library
Aberdeen, MS 39730

Lauren Rogers
Memorial Library
Box 1108
Laurel, MS 39440

Mississippi State Department
of Archives and History
Archives and Library Division
100 South State Street
Box 71
Jackson, MS 39205

University of Mississippi
Library
University, MS 38652

Missouri
Heritage Library
135 E Pine St
Warrenburg, MO 64093

Kansas City Public Library
311 E 12th St
Kansas City, MO 64106

Kent Library
Southeast Missouri
State College
Cap Girardeau, MO 63701

Missouri Historical Society
Research Library
Jefferson Memorial Building
Forest Park
St. Louis, MO 63112

Missouri State Library
308 E High St
Jefferson City, MO 65101

Records and Archives
Office of Secretary of State
Capitol Bldg
Jefferson City, MO 65101

Riverside Regional Library
Box 389
Jackson, MO 63755

St. Louis Public Library
1301 Olive St
St. Louis, MO 63103

Springfield Public Library
Reference Department
and Shepard Room
397 E Central St
Springfield, MO 65801

Montana
Parmly Billings
Memorial Library
510 N. Broadway
Billings, MT 59101

Public Library
106 W Broadway St
Butte, MT 59701

Mansfield Library
University of Montana
Missoula, MT 59812

Montana Historical Society
Library/Archives
225 North Roberts
Helena, MT 59620

Montana State Library
930 East Lyndale Avenue
Helena, MT 59601

Public Library
Pine and Pattee Sts.
Missoula, 59801

State University Library
Missoula, MT 59801

Nebraska
Alliance Public Library
202 W 4th St
Alliance, NE 69301

Nebraska D.A.R. Library
202 W 4th St
Alliance, NE 69301

Nebraska State
Historical Society Library
1500 R St
Box 82554
Lincoln, NE 68501

Omaha Public Library
215 S 15th St
Omaha, NE 68102

Public Library
136 S 14th St
Lincoln, NE 68508

University of Nebraska Library
Lincoln, NE 68503

Wayne Public Library
410 Main St.
Wayne, NE 68787

Nevada
Las Vegas Public Library
400 E Mesquite Ave
Las Vegas, NV 89101

Nevada State Historical Society
Library
P.O. Box 1192
Reno, NV 89501

Nevada State Library
and Archives
Capitol Complex
Carson City, NV 89710

University of Nevada Library
Reno, NV 89507

187

Washoe County Library
Reno, NV 89507

New Hampshire
City Library
Carpenter Memorial Bldg
405 Pine St
Manchester, NH 03104

Dartmouth College Archives
Baker Memorial Library
Hanover, NH 03755

Dover Public Library
73 Locust St
Dover, NH 03820

Exeter Public Library
86 Front St.
Exeter, NH 03833

New Hampshire State Library
20 Park St
Concord, NH 03303

New Jersey
Atlantic City Free Library
Illinois and Pacific
Atlantic City, NJ 08401

Morris Genealogical Library
228 Elberton Ave
Allenhurst, NJ 07711

New Jersey State Library
Archives and History Bureau
185 W State St
Trenton, NJ 08625

New Jersey Historical Society
Library
230 Broadway
Newark, NJ 07104

Rutgers University Library
New Brunswick, NJ 08903

New Mexico
History Library Museum
of New Mexico
Palace of the Governors
Santa Fe, NM 87501

New Mexico State
Library Commission
301 Don Gasper
Santa Fe, NM 87501

New Mexico State
Records Center and Archives
404 Montezuma Street
Santa Fe, NM 87503

Public Library
Albuquerque, NM 87501

University of New Mexico
Library
Albuquerque, NM 87106

New York
Adriance Memorial Library
93 Market St
Poughkeepsie, NY 12601

Buffalo and Erie County
Public Library
Lafayette Square
Buffalo, NY 14203

Columbia University
Journalism Library
New York, NY 10027

Flower Memorial Library
Genealogical Committee
Watertown, NY 13601

188

James T. Olin Library
Cornell University
Ithaca, NY 14851

New York Public Library
United States History,
Local History
and Genealogy Division
5th Ave and 42nd Sts.
Room 315N
New York, NY 10018

New York State
Historical Association Library
Lake Road
Box 800
Cooperstown, NY 13326

New York State Library
Albany, NY 12224

New York-Ulster County
Elting Library
Historical and
Genealogical Department
93 Main Street
New Paltz, NY 12561

Queens Borough
Public Library
89-11 Merrick Blvd
Jamaica, NY 11432

Rochester Public library
Local History Division
115 South Avenue
Rochester, NY 14604

Roswell P. Flower
Genealogy Library
229 Washington St
Watertown, NY 13601

Syracuse Public Library
335 Montgomery St
Syracuse, NY 13202

North Carolina
North Carolina State Library
109 E. Jones St.
Raleigh, NC 27611

Public Library of Charlotte
and Mecklenburg Counties
310 N Tryon St
Charlotte, NC 28202

Rowan Public Library
201 W Fisher St
Salisbury, NC 28144

University of North Carolina,
Chapel Hill
CB 3930 Wilson Library
Chapel Hill, NC 27599-3930

North Dakota
Public Library
Fargo, ND 58102

Public Library
Grand Forks, ND 58201

Public Library
516 2nd Ave
Minot, ND 58701

State Library
Bismarck, ND 58501

University of North Dakota
Library
Grand Forks, ND 58201

189

Ohio

Akron Public Library
55 S Main St
Akron, OH 44309

American Jewish Archives
Hebrew Union College
Clifton Ave
Cincinnati, OH 45220

Cincinnati Public Library
800 Vine St
Cincinnati, OH 45202

Cleveland Public Library
325 Superior Ave
Cleveland, OH 44114

Dayton and Montgomery
Counties Public Library
215 E 3rd St
Dayton, OH 45406

Ohio Historical Society Library
1985 Velma Avenue
Columbus, OH 43211

Ohio State Library
65 South Front St
Columbus, OH 43215

Portsmouth Public Library
1220 Gallia St
Portsmouth, OH 45662

Public Library of Cincinnati
and Hamilton County
8th and Vine Sts.
Cincinnati, OH 45202

Public Library of Columbus
96 S Grant Ave
Columbus, OH 43215

Public Library of Youngstown
305 Wick Ave
Youngstown, OH 44503

Toledo Public Library
Historical and Genealogical
Department
325 Michigan St
Toledo, OH 43624

University of Cincinnati
Library
Cincinnati, OH 45221

Warder Public Library
137 E High St
Springfield, OH 45502

Wayne County Public Library
304 N. Market St.
Wooster, OH 44691

Oklahoma

Carnegie Public Library
Fifth and B St
Lawton, OK 73501

Metropolitan Library System
131 Dean McGee Ave.
Oklahoma City, OK 73102

Oklahoma State Department
of Libraries
200 NE 18th St.
Oklahoma City, OK 73105

Oklahoma City Library
109 Capitol
Oklahoma City, OK 73105

Public Library
Muskogee, OK 74401

Public Library
220 S Cheyenne
Tulsa, OK 74103

State D.A.R. Library
Historical Bldg
Oklahoma City, OK 73105

Tulsa Central Library
400 Civic Center
Tulsa, OK 74103

University of Oklahoma
Library
Norman, OK 73069

Oregon
Astoria Public Library
450 10th St.
Astoria, OR 97103

City Library
100 West 13th Avenue
Eugene, OR 97401

Oregon State Archives
1005 Broadway NE
Salem, OR 97301

Oregon State Library
State Library Bldg
Summer and Count St
Salem, OR 97310

Portland Library Association
801 SW 10th Ave
Portland, OR 97205

University of Oregon Library
Eugene, OR 97403

Pennsylvania
Altoona Public Library
"The Pennsylvania Room"
1600 5th Ave
Altoona, PA 16602

Carnegie Library
4400 Forbes Ave
Pittsburgh, PA 15213

Centre County Library
203 N Allegheny St
Bellefonte, PA 16823

Citizens Library
55 S College St
Washington, DC 15301

Fackenthall Library
Franklin and Marshall College
Lancaster, PA 17602

Franklin Institute Library
Benjamin Franklin Parkway
and 20th St
Philadelphia, PA 19103

Free Library of Philadelphia
Logan Square
Philadelphia, PA 19141

Friends Library
Swarthmore, PA 19081

Historical Society
of Pennsylvania Library
1400 Locust Street
Philadelphia, PA 19107

Lutheran Historical Society
Library
Gettysburg, PA 17325

191

Lutheran Theological
Seminary Library
Mt Airy
Philadelphia, PA 19119

Pennsylvania Historical
and Museum Commission
Division of Archives
Box 1026
Harrisburg, PA 17108

Pennsylvania State Library
Walnut and Commonwealth
Harrisburg, PA 17126

Reading Public Library
Fifth and Franklin Sts.
Reading, PA 19607

University Library
Pennsylvania State University
University Park, PA 16802

Rhode Island
Providence Public Library
229 Washington St
Providence, RI 02903

Rhode Island Historical Society
Library
121 Hope Street
Providence, RI 02903

Rhode Island State Archives
314 State House
Providence, RI 02900

Rhode Island State Library
82 Smith
State House
Providence, RI 02903

South Carolina
Abbeville-Greenwood
Regional Library
N. Main St.
Greenwood, SC 29646

Free Library
404 King St
Charleston, SC 29407

Greenville County Library
300 College St
Greenville, SC 29601

Public Library
Rock Hill, SC 29730

Public Library
South Pine St
Spartanburg, SC 29302

Richland County Public Library
1400 Sumter St
Columbia, SC 29201

South Carolina Archives
Department
1430 Senate St
Columbia, SC 29201

South Carolina Library
University of South Carolina
Columbia, SC 29208
South Carolina State Library
1500 Senate St
Columbia, SC 29201

South Carolina
State Department of Archives
and History
Archives Search Room
Capitol Station, Box 11669
Columbia, SC 29211

South Dakota
Alexander Mitchell
Public Library
519 South Kline St.
Aberdeen, SD 57401

Carnegie Free Public Library
10th and Dakota St
Sioux Falls, SD 57102

South Dakota
State Historical Library
800 Governors Drive
Pierre, SD 57501-2294

University of South Dakota
Library
Vermillion, SD 57069

Tennessee
Chattanooga Hamilton County
Bicenteniel Library
Genealogy/Local History
Department
1001 Broad St
Chattanooga, TN 37402

Cossitt-Goodwyn Library
33 S Front St
Memphis, TN 38103
East Tennessee
Historical Center
500 W. Church Ave.
Knoxville, TN 37902

Memphis Public Library
1850 Peabody
Memphis, TN 38104

Memphis State University
Library
Mississippi Valley Colection
Memphis, TN 38104

Public Library of Knox County
McClung Historical Collection
600 Market St
Knoxville, TN 37902

Public Library of Nashville
and Davidson County
222 8th Ave, North
Nashville, TN 37203

Tennessee State Library
and Archives
403 7th Ave North
Nashville, TN 37219

Texas
Amarillo Public Library
300 East 4th
P.O. Box 2171
Amarillo, TX 79189

Catholic Archives to Texas
1600 Congress Ave
Austin, TX 78801

Clayton Library
for Genealogical Research
5300 Caroline
Houston, TX 77004
Dallas Public Library
Genealogy Section
1515 Young Street
Dallas, TX 75201

El Paso Genealogical Library
3651 Douglas
El Paso, TX 79903

El Paso Public Library
501 N Oregon St
El Paso, TX 79901

Fort Worth Public Library
300 Taylor St
Fort Worth, TX 76102

Genealogical Research Library
4524 Edmonson Ave
Dallas, TX 75205

Houston Public Library
500 McKinney Ave
Houston, TX 77002

San Antonio Public Library
203 S. St. Mary's St
San Antonio, TX 78205

Texarkana Public Library
901 State Line Ave
Texarkana, TX-AR 75501

Texas State Library
1201 Brazos St
Austin, TX 78711

Waco Public Library
1717 Austin Ave
Waco, TX 76701

Utah
American Genealogical
Lending Library
Box 244
Bountiful, UT 84010

Brigham Carnegie Library
26 E Forest
Brigham City, UT 84302

Brigham Young University
Library
Provo, UT 84601

Genealogical Library
Genealogical Society
of the Church of Jesus Christ
of Latter Day Saints
35 North West Temple
Salt Lake City, UT 84150

Logan Public Library
255 N. Main
Logan, UT 84321

Ogden Public Library
Ogden, UT 84402

University of Utah Library
Salt Lake City, UT 84112

Utah State Historical Society
Library
300 Rio Grande
Salt Lake City, UT 84101

Utah State University Library
Logan, UT 84321

Vermont
Billings Library
Burlington, VT 05401
Genealogical Library
Bennington Museum
Bennington, VT 05201

Public Library
Court St
Rutland, VT 05701

The Russel Collection
c/o The Dorothy Canfield
Library
Main Street
Arlington, VT 05250

University of Vermont Library
Burlington, VT 05401

Vermont Department of
Libraries, Law and Documents
111 State St
Montpelier, VT 05602

Vermont Historical Society
Library
Pavilion Office Bldg
109 State St
Montpelier, VT 05602

Virginia
Albermarle County
Historical Library
220 Court Square
Charlottesville, VA 22901

Alderman Library
University of Virginia
Charlottesville, VA 22903

Alexandria Library
717 Queen St.
Alexandria, VA 22314

College of William and Mary
Library
Williamsburg, VA 23185

Commonwealth of Virginia
Virginia State Library
1101 Capitol
Richmond, VA 23219

E. Lee Trinkle Library
University of Virginia
Fredericksburg, VA 22402

Jones Memorial Library
2311 Memorial Ave.
Lynchburg, VA 24501

Kirn Norfolk Public Library
301 E City Hall Ave
Norfolk, VA 23510

Menno Simons Historical Library
Eastern Mennonite College
Harrisonburg, VA 22801

National Genealogical Society
Library
4527 Seventeenth Street, North
Arlington, VA 22207-2363

Virginia Historical Library
P.O. Box 7311
Richmond, VA 23221

Virginia State Library
11th St. at Capitol Square
Richmond, VA 23219-3491

Washington
Olympia Timberland Library
8th and Franklin
Olympia, WA 98501
Public Library
P.O. Box 1197
Bellingham, WA 98225

Seattle Public Library
4th and Madison
Seattle, WA 98104

Spokane Public Library
W 906 Main Ave
Spokane, WA 99201

University of Washington
Library
Seattle, WA 98105

Washington State
Historical Society Library
State Historical Bldg
315 North Stadium Way
Tacoma, WA 98403

Washington State Library
State Library Bldg
Olympia, WA 98504-0111

West Virginia
Cabell County Public Library
900 5th Ave
Huntington, WV 25701

Department of Archives
and Historical Library
Cultural Center
Capitol Complex
State of West Virginia Library
Charleston, WV 25305

Morgantown Public Library
373 Spruce St
Morgantown, WV 26505

West Virginia and Regional
History Collection
Colson Hall

West Virginia University
Library
Morgantown, WV 26506

Wisconsin
Beloit Public Library
409 Pleasant St
Beloit, WI 53511

Local History
and Genealogical Library
Racine County
Historical Society
701 South Main Street
Racine, WI 53403

Milwaukee Public Library
814 W Wisconsin Ave
Milwaukee, WI 53202

State Historical Society
of Wisconsin Library
816 State Street
Madison, WI 53706-1482

University of Wisconsin
Milwaukee Library
P.O. Box 604
Milwaukee, WI 53211

Wyoming
Cheyenne Genealogical Society
Laramie County Library
Central Ave
Cheyenne, WY 82001

Western History
and Archives Department
University of Wyoming
Laramie, WY 82070

Wyoming State Archives,
Museum and Historical
Department
Barrett Building
Cheyenne, WY 82002-0130

Wyoming State Library
Supreme Court
and State Library Bldg
Cheyenne, WY 82002

Genealogical and Historical Societies

Alabama

Alabama Genealogical Society
AGS Depository
and Headquarters
Samford University Library
800 Lakeshore Dr.
Birmingham, AL 35229

Baldwin County
Genealogical Society
P.O. Box 501
Lillian, AL 36549

Birmingham
Genealogical Society
Box 2432
Birmingham, AL 35201

Butler County
Historical Society
P.O. Box 526
Greenville, AL 36037

Civil War Descendants Society
P.O. Box 233
Athens, AL 35611

East Alabama
Genealogical Society
c/o Mrs. J. H. Strothan
Drawer 1351
Auburn, AL 36830

Mobile Genealogical Society
Box 6224
Mobile, AL 36606

Alaska

Anchorage Genealogy Society
Box 100412
Anchorage, AK 99510

Fairbanks, Alaska
Genealogical Society
P.O. Box 60534
Fairbanks, AK 99706

Arizona

Arizona Genealogical Society
6521 East Fayette St.
Tucson, AZ 85730-2220

Arizona
Jewish Historical Society
4181 E. Pontatoc Canyon Dr.
Tucson, AZ 85718

Arizona State
Genealogical Society
Box 42075
Tucson, AZ 85733-2075

Genealogical Society
of Arizona
P.O. Box 27237
Tempe, AZ 85282

Phoenix Genealogical Society
4607 W. Rovey Ave.
Glendale, AZ 85301

Arkansas

Ark-La-Tex
Genealogical Assn., Inc.
P.O. Box 4462
Shreveport, LA 71104

Arkansas Genealogical Society
P.O. Box 908
Hot Springs, AK 71092

Faulkner County
Historical Society
Conway, AR 72032

Hempstead County
Historical Society
P.O. Box 1257
Hope, AR 71801

Madison County
Genealogical Society
P.O. Box 427
Huntsville, AR 72740

Northeast Arkansas
Genealogical Association
314 Vine Street
Newport, AR 73112

Northwest Arkansas
Genealogical Society
P.O. Box K
Rogers, AR 72756

Pulaski County
Historical Society
P.O. Box 653
Little Rock, AR 72203

California
California Genealogical Society
P.O. Box 77105
San Francisco, CA 94107-0105

Contra Costa County
Genealogical Society
Box 910
Concord, CA 94522

Fresno Genealogical Society
Box 1429
Fresno, CA 93716

Genealogical Society
of Riverside
Box 2557
Riverside, CA 92516

Genealogical Society
of Santa Cruz County
Box 72
Santa Cruz, CA 95063

Hi Desert Genealogical Society
15476-9 Sixth Street
Victorville, CA 92392

Historical Society of Couthern
California
200 E. Ave 43
Los Angeles, CA 90031

Jewish Genealogical Society
of Los Angeles
4530 Woodley Ave.
Encino, CA 91436

Jewish Genealogical Society
of San Diego
255 South Rios Ave.
Solana Beach, CA 92075

Kern County
Genealogical Society
Box 2214
Bakersfield, CA 93303

Los Angeles
Westside Genealogical Society
P.O. Box 10447
Marina del Rey, CA 90295

198

Mendicino County
Historical Society
603 West Perkins Street
Ukiah, CA 95482

Orange County
Genealogical Society
Box 1587
Orange, CA 92668

Paradise Genealogical Society
Box 460
Paradise, CA 95969-0460

Redwood Genealogical Society
Box 645
Fortuna, CA 95540

San Bernardino Valley
Genealogical Society
Box 26020
San Bernardino, CA 92406

San Diego Genealogical Society
2925 Kalinna Street
San Diego, CA 92104

San Francisco Bay Area
Jewish Genealogical Society
40 West 3rd Ave.
San Mateo, CA 94402

San Mateo County
Historical Association
San Mateo Junior College
San Mateo, CA 94402

Sonoma County
Genealogical Society
P.O. Box 2273
Santa Rosa, CA 95405

Southern California
Genealogical Society
P.O. Box 4377
Burbank, CA 91502

Sutter-Yuba
Genealogical Society
Box 1274
Yuba City, CA 95991

Colorado
Boulder Genealogical Society
Box 3246
Boulder, CO 80303

Colorado Genealogical Society
P.O. Box 9671
Denver, CO 80209

Colorado Historical Society
Colorado Heritage Center
1300 Broadway
Denver, CO 80203

Eastern Colorado
Historical Society
43433 Road CC
Cheyenne Wells, CO 80810

Larimer County
Genealogical Society
600 S. Shields
Fort Collins, CO 80521

Mesa County
Genealogical Society
P.O. Box 1506
Grand Junction, CO 81502

Connecticut
Brookfield, Connecticut
Historical Society
44 Hopbrook Rd.
Brookfield, CT 06804

Connecticut
Genealogical Society
P.O. Box 435
Glastonburg, CT 06033

Connecticut Historical Society
1 Elizabeth St.
Hartford, CT 06105

Jewish Genealogical Society
of Connecticut
25 Soneham Rd.
West Hartford, CT 06117

New Haven Colony
Historical Society
114 Whitney Ave.
New Haven, CT 06510

Stamford Genealogical Society
Box 249
Stamford, CT 06904

Delaware
Delaware Genealogical Society
505 Market Street Mall
Wilmington, DE 19801

Delaware Society, Sons of the
American Revolution
P.O. Box 2169
Wilmington, DE 19899

Division of Historical
and Cultural Affairs
Department of State
Hall of Records
Dover, DE 19901

District Of Columbia
Afro-American Historical
and Genealogical Society
Box 73086
Washington, D.C. 20009-3086

Jewish Genealogy Society
of Greater Washington
P.O. Box 412
Vienna, VA 22180

National Genealogical Society
4527 17th St. North
Arlington, VA 22207-2363

National Society of the
Children of the
American Revolution
1776 D Street N.W.
Washington, D.C. 20006

National Society of the
Colonial Dames of the
XVII Century
1300 New Hampshire Ave.,
N.W.
Washington, D.C. 20036

National Society of the
Daughters of the
American Revolution
1776 D Street N.W.
Washington, D.C. 20006-5392

Society of the Cincinnati
2118 Massachusetts Avenue,
N.W.
Washington, D.C. 20008

White House
Historical Association
740 Jackson Place, N.W.
Washington, D.C. 20506

Florida
Florida Genealogical Society
Box 18624
Tampa, FL 33609

Genealogical Society
of Greater Miami
P.O. Box 162905
Miami, FL 33116-2905

Hillsborough County
Historical Commission
Museum Historical
and Genealogical Library
Clunty Courthouse
Tampa, FL 33602

Jewish Genealogical Society
of Central Florida
P.O. Box 520583
Longwood, FL 32752

Manasota
Genealogical Society, Inc.
1405 4th Ave West
Bradenton, FL 34205

Palm Beach County
Genealogical Society
Box 1746
W. Palm Beach, FL 33402

Polk County
Genealogical Society
Box 1719
Bartow, FL 33830

Polk County
Historical Association
P.O. Box 2749
Bartow, FL 33830-2749

Southern Genealogist's
Exchange Society
Box 2801
Jacksonville, FL 32203

Georgia
Central Georgia
Genealogical Society
P.O. Box 2024
Warner Robbins, GA 31093

Chattahoochee Valley
Historical Society
1213 Fifth Aveune
West Point, GA 31833

Georgia Genealogical Society
Box 38066
Atlanta, GA 30334

Northeast Georgia Historical
and Genealogical Society
P.O. Box 907039
Gainesville, GA 30503-0901

Hawaii
Hawaii Society, Sons of the
American Revolution
1564 Pikea St.
Honolulu, HI 96818

Hawaiian Historical Society
560 Kawaiahao St.
Honolulu, HI 96813

Idaho
Idaho Genealogical Society
P.O. Box 326
302 North Meadow
Grangeville, ID 83530

Idaho Historical Society
325 State St.
Boise, ID 83702

Nez Perce Historical Society
P.O. Box 86
Nez Perce, ID 83542

Illinois
Bloomington-Normal
Genealogical Society
Box 488
Normal, IL 61761-0488

Chicago Genealogical Society
P.O. Box 1160
Chicago, IL 60690

Chicago Historical Society
North Ave. and Clark St.
Chicago, IL 60614

Cumberland and Coles County
Genealogical Society
Rt. 1, Box 141
Toledo, IL 62468

Decatur Genealogical Society
Box 2205
Decatur, IL 62526

Genealogical Society
of Southern Illinois
c/o Logan College
Carterville, IL 62918

Great River
Genealogical Society
c/o Quincy Public Library
Quincy, IL 62302

Illiana Genealogical Society
Box 207
Danville, IL 61832

Illinois State
Genealogical Society
P.O. Box 10195
Springfield, IL 62791

Iroquois County
Genealogical Society
Old Courthouse Museum
103 W. Cherry St.
Watseka, IL 60970

Jewish Genealogical Society
of Illinois
818 Mansfield Court
Schaumburg, IL 60194

Knox County
Genealogical Society
Box 13
Galesburg, IL 61402-0013

Lexington
Genealogical Society
304 N. Elm St.
Lexington, IL 61753

Moultrie County
Genealogical Society
Box MM
Sullivan, IL 61951

Peoria Genealogical Society
Box 1489
Peoria, IL 61655

Peoria Historical Society
942 N.E. Glen Oak Ave.
Peoria, IL 61600

Sangamon County
Genealogical Society
Box 1829
Springfield, IL 62705

Indiana
Delaware County
Historical Alliance
P.O. Box 1266
Muncie, IN 47308

Elkhart County
Genealogical Society
1812 Jeanwood Drive
Elkhart, IN 46514

Genealogical Section of the
Indiana Historical Society
140 N. Senate Ave.
Indianapolis, IN 46204

Indiana Genealogical Society
P.O. Box 10507
Anderson, IN 46852

Indiana Historical Society
315 W. Ohio Street
Indianapolis, IN 46202

Marion County
Historical Society
140 N. Senate
Indianapolis, IN 46204

Pulaski County
Genealogical Society
RR 1
Winamac, IL 46996

Iowa
Des Moines County
Genealogical Society
P.O. Box 493
Burlington, IA 52601

Iowa Genealogical Society
Box 7735
Des Moines, IA 50322

Lee County
Genealogical Society
Box 303
Keokuk, IA 52632

State Historical Society of Iowa
600 E. Locust
Des Moines, IA 50319

Kansas
Douglas County
Historical Society
Watkins Community Museum
1047 Massachusetts St.
Lawrence, KS 66044

Finney County
Genealogical Society
P.O. Box 592
Garden City, KS 67846

203

Fort Hayes Kansas
College Library
Hays, KS 67601

Heritage Genealogical Society
P.O. Box 73
Neodeska, KS 66757

Johnson County
Genealogical Society
P.O. Box 8057
Shawnee Mission, KS 66208

Kansas Genealogical Society
P.O. Box 103
Dodge City, KS 67801

Kansas State Historical Society
Memorial Bldg.
Topeka, KS 66603

Montgomery County
Genealogical Society
Box 444
Coffeyville, KS 67337

Osborne County Genealogical
and Historical Society
Osborne Public Library
Osborne, KS 67473

Riley County
Genealogical Society
2005 Claflin Road
Manhattan, KS 66502

Topeka Genealogical Society
P.O. Box 4048
Topeka, KS 66604-0048

Kentucky
Central Kentucky
Genealogical Society
Box 153
Frankfort, KY 40601

Jewish Genealogical Society
of Louisville
Annette and Milton Russman
3304 Furman B.vd.
Louisville, KY 40220

Kentucky Genealogical Society
P.O. Box 153
Frankfurt, KY 40602

Kentucky Historical Society
P.O. Box H
Frankfort, KY 40602-2108

Louisville Genealogical Society
P.O. Box 5164
Louisville, KY 40205

West-Central Kentucky Family
Research Association
P.O. Box 1932
Owensboro, KY 42302

Louisiana
Central Louisiana
Genealogical Society
P.O. Box 12206
Alexandria, LA 71315-2006

Genealogical Research Society
of New Orleans
Box 51791
New Orleans, LA 70150

204

Louisiana Genealogical
and Historical Society
Box 3454
Baton Rouge, LA 70821

North Louisiana
Genealogical Society
P.O. Box 324
Ruston, LA 71270

Maine
Maine Genealogical Society
P.O.Box 221
Farmington, ME 04938

Maine Historical Society
485 Congress St.
Portland, ME 04111

Old York Historical Society
P.O. Box 312
York, ME 03909

Maryland
Allegany County
Historical Society
218 Washington St.
Cumberland, MD 21502

Genealogical Club
of the Montgomery County
Historical Society
103 W. Montgomery Ave.
Rockville, MD 20850

Jewish Historical Society
of Maryland
15 Lloyd St.
Baltimore, MD 21202

Maryland Genealogical Society
201 West Monument St.
Baltimore, MD 21201

Massachusetts
American Jewish
Historical Society
2 Thornton Rd.
Waltham, MA 02154

Massachusetts
Historical Society
1154 Boylston St.
Boston, MA 02215

New England Historic
and Genealogical Society
101 Newberry St.
Boston, MA 02116

Winchester Historical Society
1 Copley Street
Winchester, MA 01890

Michigan
Detroit Society
for Genealogical Research
Detroit Public Library
5201 Woodward Ave.
Detroit, MI 48202

Flint Genealogical Society
P.O. Box 1217
Flint, MI 48501

Genealogical Association
of Southwestern Michigan
Box 573
St. Joseph, MI 49085

Jewish Genealogical Society
of Michigan
4987 Bantry Drive
West Bloomfield, MI 48322

Kalamazoo Valley
Genealogical Society
P.O. Box 4051
Kalamazoo, MI 49041

Mid-Michigan
Genealogical Society
3800 Glasgow Dr.
Lansing, MI 48910

Michigan
Genealogical Council
Liaison Office
Library of Michigan
717 W. Allegan
Lansing, MI 48909

Michigan
Historical Commission
505 State Office Bldg.
Lansing, MI 48913

Muskegon County
Genealogical Society
Hackley Library
316 W. Webster Ave.
Muskegon, MI 49440

Saginaw Genealogical Society
c/o Saginaw Public Library
505 Janes Ave.
Saginaw, MI 48507

Western Michigan
Genealogical Society
Grand Rapids Public Library
Grand Rapids, MI 49503

Minnesota
Anoka County
Genealogical Society
1900 3rd Ave.
Anoka, MN 55303

Minnesota
Genealogical Society
P.O. Box 16069
St. Paul, MN 55116

Minnesota Historical Society
690 Cedar St.
St. Paul, MN 55101

Range Genealogical Society
Box 388
Buhl, MN 55768

Mississippi
Mississippi
Genealogical Society
P.O. Box 5301
Jackson, MS 39216

Northeast Mississippi
Historical and Genealogical
Society
P.O. Box 434
Tupeol, MS 38801

Vicksburg
Genealogical Society, Inc.
104 Evelyn St.
Vicksburg, MS 39180

Missouri
The Heart of America
Genealogical Society
c/o Missouri Valley Rm.
Kansas City Public Library
311 E. 21st St.
Kansas City, MO 64106

Missouri Genealogical Society
P.O. Box 382
St. Joseph, MO 64502

Missouri Historical Society
Jefferson Memorial Building
Forest Park
St. Louis, MO 63112

Missouri State
Genealogical Association
P.O. Box 833
Columbia, MO 65205-0833

Ozarks Genealogical Society
Box 3494
Springfield, MO 64804

St. Louis Genealogical Society
1695 S. Brentwood Blvd.
Suite 203
St. Louis, MO 63144

West Central Missouri
Genealogical Society
705 Broad St.
Warrensburg, MO 64093

The State Historical Society
of Missouri
1020 Lowry Street
Columbia, MO 65201

Montana
Lewis and Clark County
Genealogical Society
P.O. Box 5313
Helena, MT 59604

Montana Historical Society
225 N. Roberts St.
Helena, MT 59620

Montana State
Genealogical Society
P.O. Box 555
Chester, MT 59522

Nebraska
Fort Kearny
Genealogical Society
Box 22
Kearny, NE 68847

Greater Omaha
Genealogical Society
P.O. Box 4011
Omaha, NE 68104

Madison County
Genealogical Society
Box 347
Norfolk, NE 68701

Nebraska State
Genealogical Society
P.O. Box 5608
North Platte, NE 68505

North Platte
Genealogical Society
P.O. Box 1452
North Platte, NE 69101

Nevada
Clark County, Nevada
Genealogical Society
P.O. Box 1929
Las Vegas, NV 89125-1929

Jewish Genealogical Society
of Las Vegas
P.O. Box 29342
Las Vegas, NV 89126

Nevada State
Genealogical Society
P.O. Box 20666
Reno, NV 89515

New Hampshire
Historical Society
of Chesire County
P.O. Box 803
Keene, NH 03431

New Hampshire
Historical Society, Library
30 Park Street
Concord, NH 03301

New Hampshire
Society of Genealogists
Strafford County Chapter
P.O. Box 633
Exeter, NH 03833

New Jersey
Genealogical Society
of New Jersey
P.O. Box 1291
New Brunswick, NJ 08903

Jewish Genealogical Society
of North Jersey
1 Bedford Road
Pompton Lakes, NJ 07442

New Jersey Historical Society
230 Broadway
Newark NJ 07014

New Mexico
New Mexico
Genealogical Society
Box 8283
Albuquerque, NM 87198-8330

New Mexico
Jewish Historical Society
1428 Miracerros South
Santa Fe, NM 87501

Southern New Mexico
Genealogical Society
P.O. Box 2563
Las Cruces, NM 88004

New York
Albany
Jewish Genealogical Society
Rabbi Don Cashman
P.O. Box 3850
Albany, NY 12203

Brooklyn Historical Society
128 Pierrepont St.
Brooklyn, NY 11201

Central New York
Genealogical Society
Box 104
Colvin Station
Syracuse, NY 13205

Colonial Dames of America
421 East 61st Street
New York, NY 10021

General Society
of Colonial Wars
122 East 58th St.
New York, NY 10022

Jewish Genealogical Society
P.O. Box 6398
New York, NY 10128

National Society of Colonial
Dames of America in the state
of New York, Library
215 East 71st Street
New York, NY 10021

New York Genealogical
and Biographical Society
122-126 East 58th Street
New York, NY 10022

New York State
Historical Association
Fenimore House
Lake Rd.
Cooperstown, NY 13326

Suffolk County
Historical Society
Riverhead
Long Island, NY 11901

Twin Tiers
Genealogical Society
P.O. Box 763
Elmira, NY 14902

Ulster County
Genealogical Society
P.O. Box 333
Hurley, NY 11443

North Carolina
Alleghany Historical-
Genealogical Society
P.O. Box 817
Sparta, NC 28675

Genealogical Society
of the Original Wilkes County
Wilkesboro, NC 28659

Jewish Genealogy Society
of Raleigh
8701 Sleepy Creek Dr.
Raleigh, NC 27612

North Carolina
Genealogical Society
Box 1492
Raleigh, NC 27602

North Carolina Society
of County and Local Historians
1209 Hill St.
Greensboro, NC 27408

North Dakota
Bismarck-Mandan
Genealogical Society
Box 485
Bismarck, ND 58501

McLean County
Genealogical Society
P.O. Box 51
Garrison, ND 58540

Mouse River Loop
Genealogy Society
Box 1391
Minot, ND 58702-1391

State Historical Society
of North Dakota
Liberty Memorial Bldg.
Bismarck, ND 58501

Ohio
Ashtabula County
Genealogical Society
Henderson Library
54 East Jefferson Street
Jefferson, OH 44047

Cincinnati Historical Society
Eden Park
Cincinnati, OH 45202

Genealogical Society
Morley Public Library
184 Phelps Street
Parinsville, OH 44077

Hardin County
Historical Society
P.O. Box 503
Kenton, Ohio 43326

Jewish Genealogical Society
of Cleveland
996 Eastlawn Dr.
Highland Heights, OH 44143

Miami Valley
Genealogical Society
Box 1364
Dayton, OH 45401

Northwestern Ohio
Genealogical Society
P.O. Box 17066
Toledo, OH 43615

Ohio Genealogical Society
419 W. 3rd Street
Mansfield, OH 44906

Wayne County
Historical Society
546 E. Bowman Street
Wooster, OH 44691

West Augusta
Genealogical Society
1510 Prairie Dr.
Belpre, OH 45714

Oklahoma
Federation of Oklahoma
Genealogical Societies
P.O. Box 26151
Oklahoma City, OK 73126

Love County Historical Society
P.O. Box 134
Marietta, OK 73448

Oklahoma
Genealogical Society
Box 12986
Oklahoma City, OK 73101

Tulsa Genealogical Society
Box 585
Tulsa, OK 74157

Oregon
ALSI Historical
and Genealogical Society, Inc.
P.O. Box 822
Waldport, OR 97394

Coos Bay Genealogical Forum
Box 1067
Coos Bay, OR 97459

Genealogical Forum of Portland
1410 S.W. Morrison, Rm. 812
Portland, OR 97205

Jewish Genealogical Society
of Oregon
7335 SW Linette Way
Beaverton, OR 97007

Klmath Basin
Genealogical Society
155 Hope St.
Klamath Falls, OR 97603

Mt. Hood Genealogical Forum
Box 208
Oregon City, OR 97045

Oregon Genealogical Society
P.O. Box 10306
Eugene, OR 97440-2306

Rogue Valley
Genealogical Society
125 S. Central Avenue
Medford, OR 97501

Williamette Valley
Genealogical Society
Box 2083
Salem, OR 97308

Pennsylvania
Adams County Pennsylvania
Historical Society
P.O. Box 4325
Gettysburg, PA 17325

Bucks County
Genealogical Society
P.O. Box 1092
Doylestown, PA 18901

Erie County Historical Society
117 State St.
Erie PA 16501

Erie Society
for Genealogical Research
Box 1403
Erie, PA 16512

Genealogical Society
of Pennsylvania
1300 Locust Street
Philadelphia, PA 19107

Genealogical Society
of Southwestern Pennsylvania
P.O. Box 894
Washington, PA 15301

Historical Society
of Berks County
940 Centre Ave.
Reading, PA 19605

Historical Society
of Montgomery County
1654 DeKalb St.
Norristown, PA 19401

Jewish Genealogical Society
of Philadelphia
332 Harrison Ave.
Elkins Park, PA 19117

Pennsylvania German Society
Box 97
Breinigsville, PA 18031

Presbyterian Historical Society
425 Lombard St.
Philadelphia, PA 19147

Somerset County Historical
and Genealogical Society
Road 2
Box 238
Somerset, PA 15501

South Central Pennsylvania
Genealogical Society
P.O. Box 1824
York, PA 17405

Rhode Island
Newport Historical Society
82 Touro St.
Newport, RI 02840

211

Rhode Island
Genealogical Society
P.O. Box 7618
Warwick, RI 02887-7618

Rhode Island State Historical
Society
52 Power St.
Providence, RI 02906

South Carolina
South Carolina
Genealogical Association
P.O. Box 1442
Lexington, SC 29072

South Carolina
Historical Society
P.O. Box 5401
Spartanburg, SC 29304

South Dakota
Rapid City Society
for Genealogical Research
Box 1495
Rapid City, SD 57701

South Dakota
Genealogical Society
P.O. Box 655
Sioux Falls, SD 57101

Tri-State Genealogical Society
905 5th St.
Belle Fourche, SD 57717

Tennessee
East Tennessee
Historical Society
500 W. Church Ave.
Knoxville, TN 37902-2505

Mid-West Tennessee
Genealogical Society
Box 3343
Jackson, TN 38301

Morgan County Genealogical
and Historical Society
Route 2
Box 992
Wartburg, TN 37887

Tennessee Genealogical Society
Box 11249
Memphis, TN 38111-1249

Watauga Association
of Genealogists
P.O. Box 117
Johnson City, TN 37605-0117

Texas
Amarillo Genealogical Society
Amarillo Public Library
300 East 4th
Amarillo, TX 79189

Austin Genealogical Society
Box 1507
Austin, TX 78767-1507

Central Texas
Genealogical Society
1717 Austin Ave.
Waco, TX 76701

Chaparral
Genealogical Society
Box 606
Tomball, TX 77375

Dallas Genealogical Society
P.O. Box 12648
Dallas, TX 75225

East End Historical Association
P.O. Box 2424
Galveston, TX 77550

East Texas
Genealogical Society
P.O. Box 6967
Tyler, TX 75711

El Paso Genealogical Society
El Paso Main Public Library
501 N. Oregon Street
El Paso, TX 79901

Fort Worth
Genealogical Society
Box 9767
Ft. Worth, TX 76107

Hispanic Genealogical Society
P.O. Box 810561
Houston, TX 77281-0561

Houston Area
Genealogical Association
2507 Tannehill
Houston, TX 77008-3052

Jewish Genealogical Society
of Houston
P.O. Boix 980126
Houston, TX 77098

McLennan County Society
1717 Austin Ave.
Waco, TX 76701

Mesquite Genealogical Society
Box 165
Mesquite, TX 75149

Methodist Historical Society
Fondren Library
Southern Methodist University
Dallas, TX 75222

San Antonio
Genealogical Society
Box 17461
San Antonio, TX 78217-0461

Southeast Texas
Genealogical Society
c/o Tyrell Historical Library
P.O. Box 3827
Beaumont, TX 77704

Tip O'Texas
Genealogical Society
Harlingen Public Library
Harlingen, TX 78550

Utah

Genealogical Society of Utah
35 North West Temple
Salt Lake City, UT 84150

Jewish Genealogical Society
of Salt Lake City
3510 Fleetwood Drive
Salt Lake City UT 84109

St. George Genealogy Club
P.O. Box 184
St. George, UT 84770

Utah Genealogical
Association
P.O. Box 1144
Salt Lake City, UT 84110

Vermont

Burlington, Vermont
Genealogical Group
36 Franklin Square
Burlington, VT 05401

Genealogical Society
of Vermont
Westminster West, RFD 3
Putney, VT 05346

Vermont Genealogical Society
P.O. Box 422
Pittsford, VT 05763

Vermont Historical Society
Pavillon Office Building
109 State Street
Montpelier, VT 05602

Virginia

American Society of
Genealogists
2255 Cedar Lane
Vienna, VA 22180

Central Virginia
Genealogical Association
303 Farm Lane
Charlottesville, VA 22901

Fairfax Historical Society
P.O. Box 415
Fairfax, VA 22030

Genealogical Research
Institute of Virginia
P.O. Box 29178
Richmond, VA 23229

Genealogical Society
of Tidewater
P.O. Box 76
Hampton, VA 23669

Washington

Eastern Washington
Genealogical Society
Box 1826
Spokane, WA 99210

Lower Columbia
Genealogical Society
Box 472
Longview, WA 98632

North Central Washington
Genealogical Society
P.O. Box 613
Wenatchee, WA 98801

Olympia Genealogical Society
Olympia Public Library
8th and Franklin
Olympia, WA 98501

Puget Sound
 Genealogical Society
P.O. Box 601
Tracyton, WA 98393-0601

Seattle Genealogical Society
Box 549
Seattle, WA 98111

The Tacoma
Genealogical Society
Box 1952
Tacoma, WA 98401

Tri-City Genealogical Society
P.O. Box 1410
Richland, WA 99352-1410

Washington State Genealogical
Society
Box 1422
Olympia, WA 98507

Washington State Historical
Society Library
State Historical Bldg.
315 North Stadium Way
Tacoma, WA 98403

Whatcom County Washington
Genealogical Society
P.O. Box 1493
Bellingham, WA 98227-1493

West Virginia
Marion County
Genealogical Club, Inc.
Marion County Library
Monroe Street
Fairmont, WV 26554

West Virginia
Genealogy Society, Inc.
P.O. Box 172
Elkview, WV 25071

West Virginia
Historical Society
Cultural Center
Capitol Complex
Charleston, WV 25305

Wetzel County
Genealogical Society
Box 464
New Martinsville, WV 26155

Wisconsin
Milwaukee County
Genealogical Society
P.O. Box 27326
Milwaukee, WI 53202

Jewish Genealogical Society
of Milwaukee
9280 N. Fairway Dr.
Milwaukee, WI 53217

State Historical Society
of Wisconsin
University of Wisconsin
816 State St.
Madison, WI 53706

Wisconsin State
Genealogical Society
2109 20th Avenue
Monroe, WI 53566

Wyoming
Cheyenne Genealogical Society
Laramie County Library
Central Ave.
Cheyenne, WY 82001

Converse County Genealogical
Society
119 N. 9th St.
Douglas, WY 82633

Vital Records

Please be aware that the parenthetical notes indicate the date of the earliest record available at the particular location.

Alabama
(Marriage-1936; Birth and death-1908)
Center for Health Statistics
State Department
of Public Health
434 Monroe St
Montgomery, AL 36130

Alaska
(Marriage, birth, and death-1913)
Department of Health Sciences
and Social Services
Bureau of Vital Statistics
P.O. Box H-02G
Juneau, AK 99811

Arizona
(Marriage-Write to clerk of superior court in appropriate county; Birth and death-1909)
Vital Records Section
Arizona Department of Health Services
P.O. Box 3887
Phoenix, AZ 85030

Arkansas
(Marriage-1917; Birth and death-1914)
Division of Vital Records
Arkansas Department
of Health
4815 West Markham St
Little Rock, AR 72201

California
(Marriage, birth, and death-1905)
Vital Statistics Section
Department of Health Services
410 N St
Sacramento, CA 95814

Colorado
(Marriage, birth, and death-1907)
Vital Records Section
Colorado Department
of Health
4210 East 11th Ave
Denver, CO 80220

Connecticut
(Marriage, birth, and death-1897)
Vital Records
Department of Health Services
150 Washington St
Hartford, CT 06106

Delaware
(Marriage, birth, and death-1930)
Office of Vital Statistics
Division of Public Health
P.O. Box 637
Dover, DE 19903

217

District of Columbia
(Marriage)
Marriage Bureau
515 5th St NW
Washington, DC 20001

(Birth-1874; Death-1855)
Vital Records Branch
Room 3009
425 I St NW
Washington, DC 20001

Florida
(Marriage-1927; Birth-1865;
Death-1877)
Department of Health
and Rehabilitative Services
Office of Vital Statistics
1217 Pearl St
Jacksonville, FL 32202

Georgia
(Marriage-1952; Birth and
death-1919)
Georgia Department
of Human Resources
Vital Records Unit
Room 217-H
47 Trinity Ave SW
Atlanta, GA 30334

Hawaii
(Marriage, birth, and death-
1853)
Office of Health Status
Monitoring
State Department of Health
P.O. Box 3378
Honolulu, HI 96801

Idaho
(Marriage-1947; Birth and
death-1911)
Vital Statistics Unit
Idaho Department of Health
and Welfare
450 West State St
Statehouse Mail
Boise, ID 83720

Illinois
(Marriage-1962; Birth and
death-1916)
Division of Vital Records
Illinois Department
of Public Health
605 West Jefferson St
Springfield, IL 62702

Indiana
(Marriage-1958; Birth-1907;
Death-1900)
Vital Records Section
State Board of Health
1330 West Michigan St
P.O. Box 1964
Indianapolis, IN 46206

Iowa
(Marriage, birth, and death-
1880)
Iowa Department of Public
Health
Vital Records Section
Lucas Office Building
321 East 12th St
Des Moines, IA 50319

Kansas
(Marriage-1913; Birth and death-1911)
Office of Vital Statistics
Kansas State Department
of Health and Environment
900 Jackson St
Topeka, KS 66612

Kentucky
(Marriage-1958; Birth and death-1911)
Office of Vital Statistics
Department for
Health Services
275 East Main St
Frankfort, KY 40621

Louisiana
(Marriage-1946; Birth and death-1914)
Vital Records Registry
Office of Public Health
325 Loyola Ave
New Orleans, LA 70112

(City of New Orleans only; Birth-1790; Death-1803)
Bureau of Vital Statistics
City Health Department
City Hall
Civic Center
New Orleans, LA 70112

Maine
(Marriage, birth, and death-1892)
Office of Vital Records
Human Services Building
Station 11
State House
Augusta, ME 04333

Maryland
(Marriage-1951; Birth and death-1898)
Division of Vital Records
Department of Health
and Mental Hygiene
Metro Executive Building
4201 Patterson Ave
P.O. Box 68760
Baltimore, MD 21215

(City of Baltimore only; Birth and death-1875)
Bureau of Vital Records
Municipal Office Building
Baltimore, MD 21202

Massachusetts
(Marriage, birth, and death-1896)
Registry of Vital Records
and Statistics
150 Tremont St
Room B-3
Boston, MA 02111

(City of Boston only; Birth and death-1639)
City Registrar
Registry Division
Health Department
Room 705, City Hall Annex
Boston, MA 02133

Michigan
(Marriage, birth, and death-1867)
Office of the State Registrar and
Center for Health Statistics
Michigan Department
of Public Health
3423 North Logan St
Lansing, MI 48909

219

Minnesota

(Marriage-1958; Birth and death-1908)
Minnesota Department
of Health
Section of Vital Statistics
717 Delaware St SE
P.O. Box 9441
Minneapolis, MN 55440

Mississippi

(Marriage-1926; Birth and death-1912)
Vital Records
State Department of Health
2423 North State St
Jackson, MS 39216

Missouri

(Marriage-1948; Birth and death-1910)
Department of Health
Bureau of Vital Records
1730 East Elm St
P.O. Box 570
Jefferson City, MO 65102

Montana

(Marriage-1943; Birth and death-1907)
Bureau of Records
and Statistics
State Department of Health
and Environmental Sciences
Helena, MT 59620

Nebraska

(Marriage-1909; Birth and death-1904)
Bureau of Vital Statistics
State Department of Health
301 Centennial Mall South
P.O. Box 95007
Lincoln, NE 68509

Nevada

(Marriage-Write to county recorder of appropriate county;
Birth and death-1911)
Division of Health-
Vital Statistics
Capitol Complex
505 East King St #102
Carson City, NV 89710

New Hampshire

(Marriage, birth, and death-1640)
Bureau of Vital Records
Health and Human Services
Building
6 Hazen Dr
Concord, NH 03301

New Jersey

(Marriage-Write to county clerk of appropriate county;
Birth and death-1878)
State Department of Health
Bureau of Vital Statistics
South Warren and Market St
CN 370
Trenton, NJ 08

New Mexico
(Marriage-Write to county clerk of appropriate county; Birth and death-1880)
Vital Statistics
New Mexico Health Services Division
1190 St. Francis Dr
Santa Fe, NM 87503

New York
(Marriage, birth, and death-1880)
Vital Records Section
State Department of Health
Empire State Plaza
Tower Building
Albany, NY 12237

(New York City, Borough of Bronx, only; Marriage-1914; Birth and death-1898)
Bronx Bureau of Vital Records
1826 Arthur Ave
Bronx, NY 10457

(New York City, Borough of Brooklyn, only; Marriage-1866; Birth and death-1898)
Brooklyn Bureau of Vital Records
Municipal Building
Brooklyn, NY 11201

(New York City, Borough of Manhattan, only; Marriage-1866; Birth and death-1898)
Bureau of Vital Records
Department of Health
of New York City
125 Worth St
New York, NY 10016

(New York City, Borough of Queens, only; Marriage-1898)
Office of City Clerk
120-55 Queens Blvd
Kew Gardens, NY 11424)

(New York City, Borough of Queens, only; Birth and death-1898)
Queens Bureau of Vital Records
90-37 Parsons Blvd
Jamaica, NY 11432

(New York City, Borough of Staten Island, only; Marriage-1898)
City Clerk's Office
Borough Hall
St. George
Staten Island, NY 10301

(New York City, Borough of Staten Island, only; Birth and death-1898)
Staten Island Bureau of Vital Records
51 Stuyvesant Pl
St. George
Staten Island, NY 10301

North Carolina
(Marriage-1962; Birth and death-1913)
Department of Environment, Health and Natural Resources
Division of Epidemiology
Vital Records Section
225 North McDowell St
P.O. Box 27687
Raleigh, NC 27611

North Dakota

(Marriage-1925; Birth and death-1893)
Division of Vital Records
State Capital
600 East Boulevard Ave
Bismarck, ND 58505

Ohio

(Marriage-1949; Birth and death 1908)
Division of Vital Statistics
Ohio Department of Health
G-20 Ohio Department Building
65 South Front St
Columbus, OH 43266

Oklahoma

(Marriage-Write to clerk of appropriate county; Birth and death-1908)
Vital Records Section
State Department of Health
1000 Northeast 10th St
P.O. Box 53551
Oklahoma City, OK 73152

Oregon

(Marriage-1907; Birth and death-1903)
Oregon Health Division
Vital Statistics Section
P.O. Box 116
Portland, OR 97207

Pennsylvania

(Marriage-1941; Birth and death-1906)
Division of Vital Records
State Department of Health
Central Building
101 South Mercer St
P.O. Box 1528
New Castle, PA 16103

Rhode Island

(Marriage, birth, and death-1853)
Division of Vital Records
Rhode Island
Department of Health
Room 101, Cannon Building
3 Capital Hill
Providence, RI 02908

South Carolina

(Marriage-1950; Birth and death-1915)
Office of Vital Records and Public Health Statistics
South Carolina
Department of Health
and Environmental Control
2600 Bull St
Columbia, SC 29201

South Dakota

(Marriage, birth, and death-1905)
State Department of Health
Center for Health Policy
and Statistics
Vital Records
523 East Capital
Pierre, SD 57501

Tennessee
(Marriage-1945; Birth and death-1914)
Tennessee Vital Records
Department of Health
and Environment
Cordell Hull Building
Nashville, TN 37219

(City of Memphis, only; Birth-1874; Death-1848)
Shelby County
Health Department
Division of Vital Records
Memphis, TN 38105

Texas
(Marriage-Write to county clerk of appropriate county; Birth and death-1903)
Bureau of Vital Statistics
Texas Department of Health
1100 West 49th St
Austin, TX 78756

Utah
(Marriage-Write to county clerk of appropriate county; Birth and death-1905)
Bureau of Vital Records
Utah Department of Health
288 North 1460 West
P.O. Box 16700
Salt Lake City, UT 84116

Vermont
(Marriage-1857; Birth and death-1760)
Vermont Department of Health
Vital Records Section
60 Main St
Box 70
Burlington, VT 05402

Virginia
(Marriage, birth, and death-1853)
Division of Vital Records
State Health Department
P.O. Box 1000
Richmond, VA 23208

Washington
(Marriage-1968; Birth and death-1907)
Vital Records
1112 South Quince
P.O. Box 9709, ET-11
Olympia, WA 98504

West Virginia
(Marriage-1921; Birth and death-1917)
Vital Registration Office
Division of Health
State Capital Complex
Building 3
Charleston, WV 25305

Wisconsin
(Marriage-1835; Birth and death-1852)
Vital Records
1 West Wilson St
P.O. Box 309
Madison, WI 53701

Wyoming
(Marriage-1941; Birth and death-1909)
Vital Records Services
Hathaway Building
Cheyenne, WY 82002

Books Available
from Santa Monica Press

How to Win Lotteries, Sweepstakes, and Contests
by Steve Ledoux
$12.95, 224 pages

Letter Writing Made Easy!
Featuring Sample Letters
for Hundreds of Common Occasions
by Margaret McCarthy
$12.95, 224 pages

How to Find Your Family Roots
The Complete Guide
to Searching for Your Ancestors
by William Latham
$12.95, 224 pages

- -

Order Form

Send check or money order to: **Number**
Santa Monica Press   **of Copies**
P.O. Box 1076   **at $12.95**
Santa Monica, CA 90406

Title: _____   _____

Title: _____   _____

Title: _____   _____

California residents
add 8.25% sales tax   **Subtotal**   _____

                    Shipping and Handling   **$2.00**

                              Total   _____